# Down to Earth

# Bruno Latour
# Down to Earth

---

## Politics in the New Climatic Regime

Translated by Catherine Porter

polity

First published in French as *Où atterir? Comment s'orienter en politique* © Éditions La Découverte, Paris, 2017
Reprinted: 2018 (seven times), 2019

This English edition copyright © Bruno Latour, 2018

Polity Press
65 Bridge Street
Cambridge CB2 1UR, UK

Polity Press
101 Station Landing
Suite 300
Medford, MA 02155, USA

Reprinted 2018 (seven times), 2019 (five times)

ISBN-13: 978-1-5095-3056-4
ISBN-13: 978-1-5095-3057-1 (pb)

A catalogue record for this book is available from the British Library.

Library of Congress Cataloging-in-Publication Data
Names: Latour, Bruno, author.
Title: Down to earth : politics in the new climatic regime / Bruno Latour.
Other titles: O?u atterrir? English
Description: English edition. | Cambridge, UK ; Medford, MA : Polity Press, [2018] | Includes bibliographical references and index.
Identifiers: LCCN 2018009277 (print) | LCCN 2018025558 (ebook) | ISBN 9781509530595 (Epub) | ISBN 9781509530564 | ISBN 9781509530571 (pb)
Subjects: LCSH: Globalization--Political aspects. | Climatic changes--Political aspects. | Equality.
Classification: LCC JZ1318 (ebook) | LCC JZ1318 .L38413 2018 (print) | DDC 320.58--dc23
LC record available at https://lccn.loc.gov/2018009277

Typeset in 11 on 14 pt Sabon by
Servis Filmsetting Ltd, Stockport, Cheshire
Printed and bound in the United States by LSC Communications

Cover illustration: Illustration originale créée par duofluo – design graphique pour l'exposition « Globes. Architecture et sciences explorent le monde » présentée à la Cité de l'architecture et du patrimoine du 10 novembre 2017 au 26 mars 2018, Paris.
— Droite: Coupe sur le Géorama au carré Ledoyen du jardin des Champs-Élysées. Dessin paru dans « L'Illustration », 1846.
— Gauche: Brevet d'invention et de perfectionnement de 10 ans déposé le 03.02.1825 par Charles-François-Paul Delanglard pour une machine appelée géorama, propre à l'étude de la géographie. Coupe sur le Géorama © Institut national de la propriété industrielle (INPI) / 1 BA1647_8

For further information on Polity, visit our website: politybooks.com

# Contents

# Acknowledgments

A first version of this text benefited from commentary, often quite detailed, offered by Alexandra Arènes (to whom I owe the figures), Pierre Charbonnier, Deborah Danowski, Gérard de Vries, Maylis Dupont, Jean-Michel Frodon, François Gemenne, Jacques Grinevald, Émilie Hache, Graham Harman, Chantal Latour, Anne Le Strat, Baptiste Morizot, Dominique Pestre, Nikolaj Schultz, Clara Soudan, and Isabelle Stengers. I have tried to take all their comments into account.

Certain sections of this text are reproduced in "L'Europe seule. Seule l'Europe," in Benoît Hamon, Yannick Jadot, and Michel Wieworka, eds., *La politique est à nous* (Paris: Robert Laffont, 2017), pp. 269–76, and in "L'Europe refuge," in Heinrich Geiselberger, ed., *The Great Regression* (Cambridge: Polity, 2017), pp. 78–87, as well as in journal articles: "Propositions pour recaler nos GPS politiques," *Libération*, February 3, 2016, and "Comment ne pas se tromper sur Trump," *Le Monde*, December 13, 2016.

Some of my research was carried out thanks to the project "Politiques de la terre à l'époque de l'anthropocène," USPP-Sciences Po.

We've read enough books.
Jared Kushner[1]

## I.

This essay uses the occasion of Donald Trump's election on November 8, 2016, to bring together three phenomena that commentators have already noted but without always seeing their connection. Thus, they fail to see the immense political energy that could be generated by drawing them together.

In the early 1990s, right after the victory over Communism symbolized by the fall of the Berlin Wall, just as some observers were claiming that history had run its course,[2] another history was surreptitiously getting under way.

This history was initially marked by what is called "deregulation," a term that has given the word "globalization" an increasingly pejorative cast. The same period witnessed, everywhere at once, the start of an increasingly vertiginous explosion of inequalities. These two phenomena coincided with a third that is less often stressed: the beginning of a systematic effort to deny the existence of climate change – "climate" in the broad sense of the relations between human beings and the material conditions of their lives.

This essay proposes to take these three phenomena as symptoms of a single historical situation: it is as though a significant segment of the ruling classes (known today rather too loosely as "the elites") had concluded that the earth no longer had room enough for them and for everyone else.

Consequently, they decided that it was pointless to act as though history were going to continue to move toward a common horizon, toward a world in which all humans could prosper equally. From the 1980s on, the ruling classes stopped purporting to lead and began instead to shelter themselves from the world. We are experiencing all the consequences of this flight, of which Donald Trump is merely a symbol, one among others. The absence of a *common world* we can share is driving us crazy.

The hypothesis is that we can understand nothing about the politics of the last 50 years if we do not put the question of climate change and its denial front and center. Without the idea that we have entered into a New Climatic Regime,[3] we cannot understand the explosion of inequalities, the scope of deregulation, the critique of globalization, or, most importantly, the panicky desire to return to the old protections of the nation-state – a desire that is identified, quite inaccurately, with the "rise of populism."

To resist this loss of a common orientation, we shall have to come down to earth; we shall have to *land* somewhere. So, we shall have to learn how to get our bearings, how to *orient* ourselves. And to do this we need something like a *map* of the positions imposed by the new landscape within which not only the *affects* of public life but also its *stakes* are being redefined.

The reflections that follow, written with deliberate bluntness, explore the possibility that certain political affects might be channeled toward new objectives.

Since the author lacks any authority in political science, he can only offer his readers the opportunity to disprove this hypothesis and look for better ones.

Donald Trump's supporters should be thanked for having considerably clarified these questions by pressing him to announce, on June 1, 2017, America's withdrawal from the Paris Climate Accord.

What the militancy of millions of ecologists, the warnings of thousands of scientists, the actions of hundreds of industrialists, even the efforts of Pope Francis,[4] have not managed to do, Trump succeeded in doing: everyone now knows that the climate question is at the heart of all *geopolitical* issues and that it is directly tied to questions of injustice and inequality.[5]

By pulling out of the Paris Accord, Trump explicitly triggered, if not a world war, at least a war over what constitutes the theater of operations. "We Americans don't belong to the same earth as you. Yours may be threatened; ours won't be!"

The political consequences, and presumably the military consequences – or in any case the existential consequences – of what the first President Bush had predicted in 1992, in Rio, have thus been spelled out: "Our way of life is not negotiable!" There we have it. At least things are clear: no longer is there an ideal of a world common to what used to be called "the West."

A first historic event: Brexit. The country that had invented the wide-open space of the market on the sea as well as on land; the country that had ceaselessly pushed the European Union to be nothing but a huge shop; this very country, facing the sudden arrival of thousands of refugees, decided on impulse to stop playing the game of globalization. In search of an empire that had long since vanished, it is trying to pry itself away from Europe (at the price of increasingly inextricable difficulties).

A second historic event: Trump's election. The country that had violently imposed its own quite particular form of globalization on the world, the country that had defined itself by immigration while eliminating its first inhabitants, that very country has entrusted its fate to someone who promises to isolate it inside a fortress, to stop letting in refugees, to stop going to the aid of any cause that is not on its own soil, even as it continues to intervene everywhere in the world with its customary careless blundering.

The new affinity for borders among people who had advocated their systematic dismantling is already confirming the end of one concept of globalization. Two of the greatest countries of the old "free world" are saying to the others: "Our history will no longer have anything to do with yours; you can go to hell!"

A third historic event: the resumption, extension, and amplification of migrations. At the very moment when every country is experiencing the multiple threats of globalization, many are having to figure out how to welcome onto their soil millions of people – perhaps tens of millions![6] – who are driven by the cumulative action of wars, failed attempts at economic development, and climate change, to search for territory they and their children can inhabit.

Some will claim that this is a very old problem. But no: these three phenomena are simply different aspects of one and the same metamorphosis: *the very notion of soil is changing.* The soil of globalization's dreams is beginning to slip away. This is the truly new aspect of what is discreetly called the "migratory crisis."

If the anguish runs so deep, it is because each of us is beginning to feel the ground slip away beneath our feet. We are discovering, more or less obscurely, that we are all in migration toward territories yet to be rediscovered and reoccupied.

This is because of a fourth historic event, the most important and the least discussed. It took place on December 12, 2015, in Paris, just as agreement about the climate was being reached, at the end of the conference called COP21.

What counts as a measure of the event's real impact is not what the delegates decided; it is not even whether or not the agreement is carried out (the climate change deniers will do their utmost to eviscerate it); no, the crucial fact is that, on that December day all the signatory countries, even as they were applauding the success of the improbable agreement, realized with alarm that, if they all went ahead according to the terms of their respective modernization plans, there would be no planet compatible with their hopes for development.[7] They would need several planets; they have only one.

Now if there is no planet, no earth, no soil, no territory to house the Globe of globalization toward which all these countries claim to be headed, then there is no longer an assured "homeland," as it were, for anyone.

Each of us thus faces the following question: Do we continue to nourish dreams of escaping, or do we start seeking a territory that we and our children can inhabit?

Either we deny the existence of the problem, or else *we look for a place to land.* From now on, this is what divides us all, much more than our positions on the right or the left side of the political spectrum.

And this is just as true for the *old inhabitants* of the wealthy countries as it is for their *future inhabitants*. The first, because they understand that there is no planet suited for globalization and that they will have to change their ways of life completely; the second, because they have had to leave their old devastated lands: they, too, have to change their ways of life completely and learn new ones.

In other words, the migratory crisis has been generalized.

To the migrants from *outside* who have to cross borders and leave their countries behind at the price of immense tragedies, we must from now on add the migrants *from inside* who, while remaining in place, are experiencing the drama of seeing themselves *left behind by their own countries*. What makes the migratory crisis so difficult to conceptualize is that it is the symptom, to more or less excruciating degrees, of an ordeal common to all: the ordeal of finding oneself *deprived of land*.

This ordeal accounts for the relative indifference to the urgency of the situation, and it explains why we are all climate *quietists* when we hope, while doing nothing about it, that "everything will be all right in the end." It is hard not to wonder what effect the news we hear every day about the state of the planet has on our mental state. How can we not feel inwardly undone by the anxiety of not knowing how to respond?

It is this unease, at once personal and collective, that gives Trump's election its full importance; without that, we would merely be reading the script of an exceedingly mediocre TV series.

The United States had two choices: by acknowledging the extent of climate change and the immensity of its responsibility, it could finally become realistic and lead the "free world" away from the abyss, or it could plunge further into denial. Those who conceal themselves behind Trump have decided to keep America floating in dreamland a few years longer, so as to postpone coming down to earth, while leading the rest of the world into the abyss – perhaps for good.

3.

The question of landing somewhere did not occur earlier to the peoples who had decided to "modernize" the planet. It arose – ever so painfully – only for those who for four centuries had been subjected to the impact of the "great discoveries," of empires, modernization, development, and finally globalization. They knew perfectly well what it meant to find oneself deprived of land. And they even knew quite well what it meant to be chased out of one's land. They had no choice but to become experts on the question of how to survive conquest, extermination, land grabs.

The great novelty for the modernizing peoples is that this territorial question is now addressed to them as well as to the others. It is less bloody, less brutal, less detectable, perhaps, but it is indeed a matter of an extremely violent attack destined to take away the territories of those who had up to now possessed land – most often because they had taken it away from others during wars of conquest.[8]

Here is something that adds an unexpected meaning to the term "postcolonial," as though there were a family resemblance between two feelings of loss: "You have lost your territory? We have taken it from you? Well, you

7

should know that we are in the process of losing it in turn …" And thus, bizarrely, in the absence of a sense of fraternity that would be indecent, something like a new bond is displacing the classic conflict: "How have you managed to resist and survive? It would be good if we too could learn this from you."[9] Following the questions comes a muffled, ironic response: "Welcome to the club!"

In other words, the sense of vertigo, almost of panic, that traverses all contemporary politics arises owing to the fact that the ground is giving way beneath everyone's feet at once, as if we all felt attacked everywhere, in our habits and in our possessions.

Have you noticed that the emotions involved are not the same when you're asked to defend nature – you yawn, you're bored – as when you're asked to defend your territory – now you're wide awake, suddenly mobilized?

If nature has become territory, it makes little sense to talk about an "ecological crisis," "environmental problems," or a "biosphere" to be rediscovered, spared, or protected. The challenge is much more vital, more existential than that – and also much more comprehensible, because it is much more direct. When the rug is pulled out from under your feet, you understand at once that you are going to have to be concerned with the floor …

It is a question of attachment, of lifestyle, that's being pulled out from under us, a question of land, of property giving way beneath us, and this uneasiness gnaws at everyone equally, the former colonizers and the formerly colonized alike. But actually, no, it upsets the former colonizers much more, as they are less accustomed to the situation than are the formerly colonized. What is certain is that all find themselves facing a universal lack of shareable space and inhabitable land.

But where does this panic come from? From the same deep feeling of injustice felt by those who found themselves deprived of their land at the time of the conquests, then during colonization, and finally during the era of "development": a power from elsewhere comes to deprive you of your land and you have no purchase on that power. If this is globalization, then we understand retrospectively why resisting it has always been the only solution, why the colonized have always been right to defend themselves.

This is the new way in which we can experience the universal human condition – a wicked universality, to be sure, but the only one available to us, now that the previous universality, promised by globalization, seems to be receding from the horizon. The new universality consists in feeling that the ground is in the process of giving way.

Isn't this new universality enough to allow us to understand one another and prevent future wars over the appropriation of space? Probably not, but it is our only way out: discovering in common what land is inhabitable and with whom to share it.

The alternative is to act as though nothing were happening and to protect ourselves behind a wall while we prolong the waking dream of the "American way of life" – from which, as we know, what will soon be nine or ten billion humans will be unable to benefit.

Migrations, explosions of inequality, and New Climatic Regime: *these are one and the same threat.* Most of our fellow citizens underestimate or deny what is happening to the earth, but they understand perfectly well that the question of migrants puts their dreams of a secure identity in danger.

For the time being, fully aroused and worked over by the so-called "populist" parties, these citizens have grasped the ecological mutation in just one of its dimensions. The climate crisis is forcing people they do not welcome to cross their frontiers; hence the response: "Let's put up impenetrable borders and we'll escape from the invasion!"

But it is the other dimension of this same mutation that they have not yet fully grasped: the New Climatic Regime has been sweeping across all our borders for a long time, exposing us to all the winds, and no walls we can build will keep these invaders out.

If we want to defend our affiliations, we shall have to *identify* these migrations also, migrations without form or nation that we know as climate, erosion, pollution, resource depletion, habitat destruction. Even if you seal the frontiers against two-legged refugees, you cannot prevent these others from crossing over.

"But then is no one at home any longer?"

No, as a matter of fact. Neither state sovereignty nor inviolable borders can take the place of politics any longer.

"But then everything is open, we are going to have to live outside, without any protection at all, tossed about by the winds, mixed in with everyone else, fighting for everything without any more guarantees, moving around endlessly, losing all identity, all comfort! Who can live like that?"

No one, it is true. Neither a bird, nor a cell, nor a migrant, nor a capitalist. Even a Diogenes has the right to a barrel, as does a nomad to his tent, a refugee to her asylum.

Don't be fooled for a second by those who preach the call of wide-open spaces, of "risk-taking," those who abandon all protection and continue to point to the infinite horizon of modernization for all. Those good apostles take risks only if their own comfort is guaranteed. Instead of listening to what they are saying about what lies ahead, look instead at what lies behind them: you'll see the gleam of the carefully-folded golden parachutes, of everything that ensures them against the random hazards of existence.

The most basic right of all is to feel safe and protected, especially at a moment when the old protections are disappearing.

This is the meaning of the history that remains to be discovered: how can we reweave edges, envelopes, protections; how can we find new footing while simultaneously taking into account the end of globalization, the scope of migration, and also the limits placed on the sovereignty of nation-states that are henceforth confronted by climate change?

Above all, how can we reassure those who see salvation only in the recollection of a national or ethnic identity, always freshly reinvented? And, in addition, how can we organize a collective life around the extraordinary challenge of accompanying millions of foreigners in their search for lasting ground?

The political question is how to reassure and shelter all those persons who are obliged to take to the road, even while turning them away from the false protection of identities and rigid borders.

But how can they be reassured? How can these

migrants be given the feeling of being protected without relying at once on an identity based on an idea of origins, autochthonous races, secure borders, insurance against all risks?

To reassure them, we would have to be able to succeed in carrying out two complementary movements that the ordeal of modernization has made contradictory: *attaching oneself to a particular patch of soil* on the one hand, *having access to the global world* on the other. Up to now, it is true, such an operation has been considered impossible: between the two, it is said, one has to choose. It is this apparent contradiction that current history may be bringing to an end.

### 4.

What is meant, at bottom, by the ravages of globalization? It would seem that globalization is the source of all evils, that it is against globalization that the various "peoples" have suddenly "revolted" in a supreme effort of "consciousness-raising" that has, it is said, "opened their eyes" to the excesses of the "elites."

It is time to pay attention to the words we are using. In "globalize" there is a good deal of "globabble," to be sure, but there is also the word "globe," just as in Donna Haraway's "worlding" there is also the word "world." It would be a real shame to have to do without them.

For 50 years, what is called "globalization" has in fact consisted in *two opposing phenomena* that have been systematically confused.

Shifting from a local to a global viewpoint ought to mean *multiplying* viewpoints, *registering* a greater number of varieties, *taking into account* a larger number of beings, cultures, phenomena, organisms, and people.

Yet it seems as though what is meant by globalization today is the exact opposite of such an increase. The term is used to mean that *a single vision*, entirely provincial, proposed by a few individuals, representing a very small number of interests, limited to a few measuring instruments, to a few standards and protocols, has been imposed on everyone and spread everywhere. It is hardly surprising that we don't know whether to embrace globalization or, on the contrary, struggle against it.

If it is a matter of *multiplying* viewpoints so as to complicate all "provincial" or "closed" views with new variants, it is a fight that deserves to be fought. If it is a matter of *decreasing* the number of alternatives regarding the existence and the course of the world, the value of goods and the definitions of the Globe, it is clear that we have to resist such simplifications with all our might.

On balance, it seems that the more one is globalized, the more one has the impression of having a limited view! Each of us is ready to pull away from our own little plots of land, but surely not in order to be subjected to the narrow vision of another little plot that is simply farther away. So, from here on let us distinguish between globalization-*plus* and globalization-*minus*.

What is going to complicate any project of landing someplace is that this definition of the inevitable globalization will lead, in a backlash, to the invention of the "reactionary."

The advocates of globalization-minus have for a long time accused those who resist its deployment of being archaic, backward, thinking only of their own little parcels of land and seeking to protect themselves against all risks by remaining enclosed in their own little homes! (Ah! the taste for wide-open spaces preached by those who are sheltered wherever their frequent flyer miles will take them ...)

It is to stir up this backward-looking people that globalizers have subjected them to the great lever of modernization. For two centuries, the arrow of time has made it possible to locate on one side those who are moving forward – the modernizers, the progressives – and on the other those who remain behind.

The battle cry "Modernize!" has no content but this: all resistance to globalization will be immediately deemed illegitimate. There is no need to negotiate with those who want to stay behind. Those who take shelter on the other side of the irreversible forward march of globalization will be disqualified in advance.[10] They are not only defeated, they are also irrational. *Woe to the vanquished!*

Advocacy of this type of modernization defines, by contrast, the taste for the local, the attachment to the land, the maintenance of traditions, the attention to the earth. No longer treated as a set of legitimate feelings, these stances are accused of merely expressing nostalgia for "archaic" and "obscurantist" positions.

The call to globalization is so ambiguous that its pliancy contaminates what can be expected from the local. This is why, since the beginning of modernization, any attachment to any soil at all has been read as a sign of backwardness.

Just as there are two entirely different ways of viewing globalization, of registering the variations in the Globe, there are thus at least two ways, equally contrasting, to define the attachment to the local.

And here is where the elites who have so greatly profited from globalizations (-plus as much as -minus) have so much trouble understanding what upsets those who want to be held, protected, assured, reassured by their province, their tradition, their soil, or their identity. The elites accuse them of giving in to the sirens of "populism."

Refusing modernization may be a reflex born of fear, lack of ambition, inborn laziness, yes, but, as Karl Polanyi saw so clearly, society is always right in defending itself against attacks.[11] To reject modernization is also to *resist courageously* by refusing to trade one's own province for another – Wall Street, Beijing, or Brussels – that is even narrower and above all infinitely remote, thus much more indifferent to local interests.

Is it possible to make those who are still enthusiastic about globalization understand that it is normal, that it is just, that it is indispensable to want to preserve, maintain, ensure one's belonging to a land, a place, a soil, a community, a space, a milieu, a way of life, a trade, a skill? Precisely so as to remain capable of registering more differences, more viewpoints, and above all not to begin by reducing their number.

Yes, the "reactionaries" are wrong about globalization, but the "progressives" are also surely wrong about what keeps the "reactionaries" attached to their customs and habits.

Let us distinguish, consequently, the local-*minus* from the local-*plus*, just as we have to distinguish globalization-minus from globalization-plus. In the end, what counts is not knowing whether you are for or against globalization, for or against the local; all that counts is understanding whether you are managing to register, to maintain, to cherish a maximum number of alternative ways of belonging to the world.

We'll be told that this is splitting hairs and introducing artificial divisions, the better to hide some old ideology of blood and soil (*Blut und Boden*).

To offer such an objection is to forget the massive event that has intervened to put in danger the great modernization project. If the project has become impossible, it's because there is no Earth capable of containing its ideal of progress, emancipation, and development.[12] As a result, *all forms of belonging* are undergoing metamorphosis – belonging to the globe, to the world, to the provinces, to particular plots of ground, to the world market, to lands or to traditions.

We must face up to what is literally a problem of dimension, scale, and lodging: the planet is *much too narrow and limited* for the globe of globalization; at the same time, it is *too big*, infinitely too large, too active, too complex, to remain within the narrow and limited borders of any locality whatsoever. We are all overwhelmed twice over: by what is too big, and by what is too small.

And thus no one has the answer to the question "how can one find inhabitable land?" Neither the advocates of globalization (-plus as well as -minus) nor the advocates of the local (-plus as well as -minus). We don't know where to go, or how to live, or with whom to cohabit. What must we do to find a place? How are we to orient ourselves?

## 5.

Something must have happened, some truly extraordinary event, for the ideal of globalization to have changed valence so quickly. Fleshing out an earlier hypothesis with a political fiction allows us to situate this event more precisely.

Let us suppose that, from the 1980s on, more and more people – activists, scientists, artists, economists, intellectuals, political parties – have grasped the increasingly endangered status of the formerly more or less stable relations that the Earth maintained with humans.[13] Despite the difficulties, this avant-garde has managed to accumulate evidence that those stable relations could not last, that the Earth, too, would end up resisting.

Earlier, everyone saw quite clearly that the question of limits would inevitably arise, but the shared decision, among the Moderns at least, had been to ignore that question bravely by a very strange form of disinhibition.[14] One could go ahead and grab land, use it and abuse it, without listening to the prophets of doom, since the ground itself kept more or less quiet!

And yet, little by little, we find that *under* the ground of private property, of land grabs, of the exploitation of territories, *another ground*, another earth, another soil has begun to stir, to quake, to be moved. A sort of earthquake, if you like, that led the pioneers to say: "Watch out, nothing will be as it was before; you are going to have to pay dearly for the return of the Earth, the outburst of powers that had been tame until now."

And here is where the hypothesis of political fiction comes in. Suppose that other elites, perhaps less enlightened, but with significant means and important interests, and above all with extreme attentiveness to the security of their immense fortunes and to the durability of their well-being, had, each and every one of them, heard this threat, this warning.

We have to assume that these elites understood perfectly well that the warning was accurate, but did not conclude from the evidence, which had become more and more indisputable over the years, that they were going to have to pay, and pay dearly, for the Earth's turning back on itself. They would have been enlightened enough to register the warning, but not enlightened enough to share the results with the public.

On the contrary, we must suppose that they drew two consequences from the warning, which resulted in the election of the Tweeter-in-Chief to the White House. "First, yes, we shall have to pay dearly for this upheaval, but *the others are going to pay* for what is broken, certainly not we ourselves; and, secondly, as for this less and less debatable truth about the New Climatic Regime, *we are going to deny its very existence!*"

These two decisions would make it possible to connect three phenomena: what since the 1980s has been called "deregulation" or the "dismantling of the welfare state"; what since the 2000s is known as "climate-change denial"[15]; and above all, what for the last 40 years has been a dizzying extension of inequalities.[16]

If the hypothesis is correct, all this is part of a single phenomenon: the elites have been so thoroughly convinced that there would be no future life for everyone that they have decided *to get rid of all the burdens of solidarity as fast as possible* – hence deregulation; they have decided that a sort of gilded fortress would have to be built for those (a small percentage) who would be able to make it through – hence the explosion of inequalities[17]; and they have decided that, to conceal the crass selfishness of such a flight out of the shared world, they would have to reject absolutely the threat at the origin of this headlong flight – hence the denial of climate change.

To go back to the well-worn metaphor of the Titanic, the ruling classes understand that the shipwreck is certain; they reserve the lifeboats for themselves and ask the orchestra to go on playing lullabies so they can take advantage of the darkness to beat their retreat before the ship's increased listing alerts the other classes![18] For a clarifying episode that is not metaphoric in the least: Exxon-Mobil, in the early 1990s, knowing full well what it was doing, after publishing excellent scientific articles on the dangers of climate change, chose to invest massively in frenetic extraction of oil and at the same time in an equally frenetic campaign to proclaim the non-existence of the threat.[19]

These people – whom we can call the obscurantist elites from now on – understood that, if they wanted to survive in comfort, *they had to stop pretending, even in their dreams, to share the earth with the rest of the world.*

This hypothesis would make it possible to explain how globalization-plus has become globalization-minus. Whereas until the 1990s one could (provided that one profited from it) associate the horizon of modernization with the notions of progress, emancipation, wealth, comfort, even luxury, and above all rationality, the rage to deregulate, the explosion of inequalities, the abandonment of solidarities have gradually associated that horizon with the notion of an arbitrary decision out of nowhere in favor of the sole profit of the few. The best of worlds has become the worst.

Looking down from the ship's rail, the lower classes, now fully awakened, see the lifeboats pulling farther and farther away. The orchestra continues to play "Nearer, my God, to Thee," but the music no longer suffices to drown out the cries of rage ...

And it is indeed of rage that we must speak if we want to understand the reaction of defiance and incomprehension in the face of such a betrayal.

If the elites felt, starting in the 1980s or '90s, that the party was over and that they would have to build more gated communities[20] so they would no longer have to share with the masses, especially not the masses "of color" that would soon be on the move throughout the planet because they were being chased away from their homes, one can imagine that those left behind also understood very quickly that if globalization were tossed aside, then they too would need gated communities.

The reactions on one side led to reactions on the other – both sides *reacting to another much more radical reaction, that of the Earth*, which had stopped absorbing blows and was striking back with increasing violence.

This overlapping seems irrational only if we forget that we are dealing with one and the same chain reaction whose origin must be sought in the Earth's reaction to our enterprises. We are the ones who started it – we of the old West, and more specifically Europe. There are no two ways about it: we have to learn to live with the consequences of what we have unleashed.

We understand nothing about the terrifying growth in inequalities or about the "wave of populism" or the "migration crisis" if we do not understand that these are three different responses, basically comprehensible if not effective, to the powerful reaction of the Earth to what globalization has done to it.

In the face of the threat, according to our political fiction, a decision has been made not to face up to it but to flee. Some glide into the gilded exile of the 1% – "The super-rich have to be protected above all else!" – while others cling to secure borders – "Have pity, let us at least have the guarantee of a stable identity!" – and still others, the most wretched of all, take the road to exile.

In the final analysis, they are all the "left-behinds of globalization" (-minus) – which is beginning to lose its power of attraction.

### 6.

The obscurantist elites, according to this narrative, have taken the threat seriously; they have concluded that their dominance was threatened and have decided to dismantle the ideology of a planet shared by all; they have understood that such an abandonment could under no circumstances be made public, and consequently that the scientific knowledge that underlay their whole movement would have to be obliterated under conditions of the greatest secrecy – all this in the course of the last 30 or 40 years.

The hypothesis appears implausible: the idea of negation looks too much like a psychoanalytic interpretation, too much like a conspiracy theory.[21] It is not impossible to document it, however, if we make the reasonable assumption that people are fairly quick to suspect what some are seeking to hide from them, and are prepared to act accordingly.

In the absence of flagrant evidence, the effects themselves are quite visible. At the moment, the most edifying of these effects is the epistemological delirium that has taken hold of the public stage since the election of Donald Trump.

Denegation is not a comfortable situation. To deny in this fashion is to lie cold-bloodedly, and then to forget that one has lied – even while constantly remembering the lie after all. This is draining. We may well wonder, then: what does such a tangle do to the people who are caught in its net? The answer: it drives them crazy.

And in the first place this "people" that the official commentators seem suddenly to be discovering. Journalists have seized on the idea that the populus has become attached to "alternative facts" to the point of forgetting all forms of rationality.

Commentators set about accusing these good folks of complacency in their narrow vision, their fears, their inborn suspicion of elites, their deplorable indifference to the very idea of truth, and especially their passion for identity, folklore, archaism, and borders – and on top of all that, for good measure, a condemnable indifference to the facts.

Whence the success of the expression "alternative reality."

But this is to forget that this "people" *has been coldly betrayed* by those who have given up the idea of actually pursuing the modernization of the planet *with* everyone, because they knew, before everyone else, that such modernization was impossible – precisely for want of a planet vast enough for their dreams of growth for all.

Before accusing "the people" of no longer believing in anything, one ought to measure the effect of that overwhelming betrayal on people's level of trust. Trust has been abandoned along the wayside.

No attested knowledge can stand on its own, as we know very well. Facts remain robust only when they are supported by a common culture, by institutions that can be trusted, by a more or less decent public life, by more or less reliable media.[22]

And people to whom it has never been announced openly (although they suspect it) that all the efforts to modernize for the last couple of centuries are at risk of collapsing, that all ideals of solidarity have been thrown overboard by their own leaders – these people are expected to have the confidence of a Louis Pasteur or a Marie Curie in scientific facts!

But the epistemological disaster is just as great among those who are in charge of carrying out this extraordinary betrayal.

To become convinced of this, it suffices to observe on a daily basis the chaos that has reigned at the White House since Trump's arrival. How can one respect the best-established facts, when one has to deny the enormity of the threat and wage, without acknowledging it, a full-scale war against all the others? It is like cohabiting with the proverbial "elephant in the room," or with Ionesco's rhinoceros. There is nothing more uncomfortable. These big animals snore, cackle, roar, crush you, and prevent you from thinking straight. The Oval Office has become a real zoo.

For denegation poisons those who practice it as well as those who are presumed to be duped by it. (We shall look at the form of deception peculiar to "Trumpism" later on.)

The only difference, albeit a crucial one, is that the superrich, of whom Trump is merely the intermediary, have added to their flight a crime for which there is no atoning: their obsessional denial of climate change. Because of this denial, ordinary people have had to cope within a fog of disinformation, without anyone ever telling them that the project of modernizing the planet was over and done with, and that a regime change was inevitable.

Ordinary people already had a general tendency to be skeptical; now they have been incited, thanks to billions of dollars invested in disinformation, to be skeptical about one massive fact – the mutation of the climate.[23] The truth is that, if there were to be any hope of dealing with this fact in time, ordinary people would have had to have confidence in its solidity very early on, in order to push politicians to act before it was too late. At a point when the public could have found an emergency exit, the climate skeptics stood in their way and denied them access. When the time comes to judge, this is the crime for which charges will be brought.[24]

The public does not fully realize that the issue of climate-change denial organizes all politics at the present time.[25] When journalists talk about "post-truth" politics, they do so very lightly. They do not stress the reason why some have decided to keep on engaging in politics while voluntarily abandoning the link to the truth that (rightly!) terrified them. Nor do they stress the reason why ordinary people have decided – and rightly so, in their case too – not to believe in anything any longer. Given what their leaders have already tried to make them swallow, it is understandable that they are suspicious of everything and don't want to listen any more.

The reactions of the media prove that the situation is no better, alas, among those who boast of having remained "rational thinkers," who are indignant about the indifference to facts of the "Tweeter-in-Chief," or who rail about the stupidity of the ignorant masses. These "rational" folk continue to believe that facts stand up all by themselves, without a shared world, without institutions, without a public life, and that it would suffice to put the ignorant folk back in an old-style classroom with a blackboard and in-class exercises, for reason to triumph at last.

But these "rational" sorts are just as caught up as the others in the tangles of disinformation. They do not see that it is useless to be indignant that people "believe in alternative facts," when they themselves live in an alternative *world*, a world in which climate mutation occurs, while it does not in the world of their opponents.

It is not a matter of learning how to repair cognitive deficiencies, but rather of how to live in the same world, share the same culture, face up to the same stakes, perceive a landscape that can be explored in concert. Here we find the habitual vice of epistemology, which consists in attributing to intellectual deficits something that is quite simply a deficit in shared practice.


7.

If the key to the current situation cannot be found in a lack of cognitive abilities, it has to be sought in the form of the world to which those very abilities are applied.

Now here is precisely where the problem lies: there are now several worlds, several territories, and they are mutually incompatible.

To simplify, let us suppose that, up to now, all persons who had once agreed to go along with the project of modernization could now rediscover where they belong thanks to a *vector* going from the local to the global.

It is toward the Globe with a capital G that everything would begin to move, the Globe that simultaneously delineated scientific, economic, and moral horizons, the Globe of globalization-plus. A marker that was both spatial – represented by cartography – and temporal – represented by the arrow of time pointing toward the future. Carried along by this Globe, which aroused enthusiasm for generations because it was synonymous with wealth, freedom, knowledge, and access to a life of ease, was a certain definition of humanity.

At last, the open seas! At last, a way out of the confines of home! At last, the infinite universe! Very few have been immune to this appeal. Let us try to measure the enthusiasm to which it gave rise among those who profited from it – without being surprised at the horror that it arouses among those it has crushed along the way.

What had to be *abandoned* in order to modernize was the Local. This term, too, calls for a capital letter so that it won't be confused with some primordial habitat, some ancestral land, the soil from which native populations have sprung. There is nothing aboriginal, nothing native, nothing primitive in this territory reinvented *after* modernization had done away with all the old connections. It is a Local through contrast. An anti-Global.

Once these two poles have been identified, we can trace a pioneering frontier of modernization. This is the line drawn by the injunction to modernize, an injunction that prepared us for every sacrifice: for leaving our native province, abandoning our traditions, breaking with our habits, if we wanted to "get ahead," to participate in the general movement of development, and, finally, to profit from the world.

People were of course torn between two contradictory injunctions: to move forward toward the ideal of progress, or backward toward the old certainties; but this hesitation, this tug-of-war, ultimately suited them pretty well. Just as Parisians know how to determine where they are along the course of the Seine by noting the sequence of odd and even numbers in their streets, we knew how to locate ourselves in the course of history.

There were of course protestors, but they were located *on the other side* of the modernization front. They were the (neo-)natives, the antiquated, the vanquished, the colonized, the subaltern, the excluded. Thanks to that touchstone, one could treat them unassailably as reactionaries, or at least as anti-moderns, as dregs, rejects. They could certainly protest, but their whining only justified their critics.

It was brutal, perhaps, but at last the world had a direction. The arrow of time was going somewhere.

Such a positioning was all the easier in that this was the vector along which the Left/Right distinction – now in question – had been projected.

This projection was not uncomplicated, because, depending on the topics under dispute, Left and Right often went in different directions.

When the economy was in question, for example,

there was a Right that always wanted to go farther toward the Global, while there was a Left (but also a more timid Right) that would have preferred to set limits, slow down, protect the weakest against the forces of the Market (the capital letters serve as reminders that we are dealing with simple ideological markers).

Conversely, when "liberation of morals," and sexual issues in particular, were under discussion, there was always a Left that wanted to move ahead toward the Global, while there was a Right (but also a Left) that firmly refused to be dragged down that "slippery slope."

This sufficed to complicate somewhat the attribution of labels such as "progressive" and "reactionary." But one could nevertheless find true "reactionaries" – at once against the "market forces" and against the "liberation of morals" – and true "progressives," a compound of Right and Left, whose wish to free both the forces of capital and the diversity of moral standards spurred their affinity for the Global.

These subtleties aside, people ended up finding common ground in spite of everything, for the good reason that all these positions continued to be situated *along the same vector*. Which made it possible to identify them the way one reads the temperature of a patient by following the gradations of a thermometer.

The direction of history being a given, there could be obstacles, "regressions," "rapid advances," or even "revolutions" and "restorations," but no radical change in the general ordering of positions. Depending on the topics under dispute, the *import* of the positions could vary, but there was always *a single direction* that derived from the tension between the two poles of

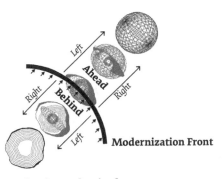

Attractor 2 – Global-of-modernization

Left

Ahead

Right

Behind

Right

Left

Modernization Front

Attractor 1 – Local-to-be-modernized

Figure 1 Canonical schema of the Moderns' orientation

attraction, the Global and the Local. (Once again, these are only convenient abstractions.)

As the matter is going to become complicated very quickly, a schematic rendering will be useful. The canonical form (figure 1) allows us to situate the Local-to-be-modernized and the Global-of-modernization as two *poles of attraction* labeled attractor 1 and attractor 2. Between the two, there is the modernization front that clearly distinguishes between what is ahead and what is behind, as well as the projection along this vector of the various ways of being associated with the Right or the Left, necessarily simplified.

This particular pairing of Global and Local obviously leaves out all the other ways of being local and global that have been revealed to us by anthropology but that remain invisible to the Moderns and thus do not belong to the schema – at least for now. To be modern, by definition, is to project onto the others at every turn the conflict between the Local and the Global, between the archaic past and the future – a future with which the non-moderns, it goes without saying, have nothing to do.[26]

(To be complete, we would need to add an infinite extension to the project of attractor 2, to accommodate those who want to escape from the problems of the planet by moving to Mars, or teleporting themselves into computers, or becoming truly post-human thanks to the marriage of DNA, cognitive science, and robots.[27] This extreme form of "neo-hyper-modernism" only speeds up the old vector vertiginously and is thus of no importance for what follows.)

What happens to this system of coordinates if globalization-plus becomes globalization-minus? If what has been the pole of attraction drawing us with the force of self-evidence, pulling the whole world in its direction, becomes a counterforce that pushes us away, leaving us with the confused feeling that only a few will profit from it? Inevitably, the Local, too, in a counterreaction, will become attractive again.

But at this point it is no longer the same Local. To the headlong flight toward globalization-minus there is a corresponding headlong flight toward the Local-minus, the Local that promises tradition, protection, identity, and certainty within national or ethnic borders.

And herein lies the drama: the made-over Local is no more plausible, no more livable than globalization-minus. It is a retrospective invention, a rump territory, the remains of what has been definitively left behind by modernization. What is more unreal than Kaczyński's Poland, the National Front's France, the Northern League's Italy, Brexit's shrunken Great Britain, or Trump's deceitful great-again America?

Nevertheless, this second pole attracts as powerfully as the first, especially when things are going badly and the ideal of the Globe seems to be more and more remote.

The two poles of attraction have finally pulled so far apart that we no longer have the luxury of hesitating, as before, between the two. This is what the commentators call the brutalization of political discourse.

For the modernization front to have a certain credibility, for it to organize the direction of history in a lasting way, the actors all had to live in the same place, or at least they had to have something like a common horizon, even as they were pulling in different directions.

Now those who supported globalization, like those who advocate returning to the past, have all begun to flee as quickly as possible, competing in their lack of

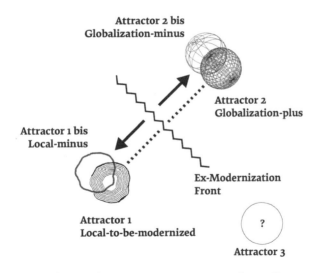

Figure 2 The Moderns' customary system of coordinates shattered by the irruption of a third attractor

realism. Bubble versus bubble; gated community versus gated community.

Instead of tension, there is henceforth a yawning gap. Instead of a front line, we see only the scar of an old battle for or against the modernization of the whole planet. There is no longer a shared horizon – even to decide who is progressive and who is reactionary.[28]

People find themselves in the situation of passengers on a plane that has taken off for the Global, to whom the pilot has announced that he has had to turn around because one can no longer land at that airport, and who then hear with terror ("Ladies and gentlemen, this is the captain speaking again") that the emergency landing strip, the Local, is also inaccessible. It is understandable that these passengers would press against the plane's windows to try to see where they are going to be able to attempt a crash landing – even if they are counting, as in Clint Eastwood's film, on the reflexes of a Captain Sully.[29]

So, what has actually happened? We have to suppose that something has come to twist the arrow of time, some at once ancient and unexpected power that initially worried, then disturbed, and finally dispersed the projects of the aforementioned Moderns. It is as if the expression modern *world* had become an oxymoron. Either it is modern, but has no world under its feet, or else it is a true world, but will not be modernizable. We have reached the end of a certain historical arc.

Abruptly, it is as though, everywhere at once, a *third pole of attraction* has come in to turn aside, pump out, absorb all the objects of conflict, making any orientation along the old flight line impossible.

And it is at this point in history, at this juncture, that we find ourselves today. Too disoriented to array the positions along the axis that went from the old to the new, from the Local to the Global, but still incapable of naming this third attractor, fixing its position, or even simply describing it.

And yet the entire political orientation depends on this step to the side: we shall really have to decide who is helping us and who is betraying us, who is our friend and who is our enemy, with whom we should make alliances and with whom we should fight – but while taking a direction that is no longer mapped out.

There is nothing, in any case, that authorizes us to re-use the old markers such as "Right" and "Left," "liberation," "emancipation," "market forces." Or even the markers of space and time that have appeared self-evident for so long, such as "Local" or "Global," "future" or "past."

Everything has to be mapped out anew, at new costs. What is more, this is an urgent task that must be carried out before the sleepwalkers, in their blind headlong rush forward, have crushed what we care about.

### 8.

If it could be claimed, at the beginning of this text, that the US decision to withdraw from the Paris Climate Accord clarified the new political situation, it was because the idea behind the course proposed is so *diametrically opposed* to the direction that ought to be taken that it defines quite well, but by contrast, the position of this third attractor!

To assess with some confidence the extent to which the situation is being clarified, it suffices to imagine the state of conversations if the Brexit campaign had failed in June 2016, if Hillary Clinton had been elected, or if after his election Trump had not withdrawn from the Paris Accord. We would still be weighing the benefits and drawbacks of globalization as if the modernization front remained intact. Fortunately, if such an adverb can be used, the events of the past year have made this still less attractive.

"Trumpism" is a political innovation of a rare sort that needs to be taken seriously.[30]

In fact, the shrewd maneuver of those who support it consisted in building a radical movement based on the systematic *denial* that climate change exists.

It is as though Trump had managed to identify a *fourth attractor*. This one is easy to name: it is the *Out-of-This-World* (figure 3), the horizon of people who no longer belong to the realities of an earth that would react

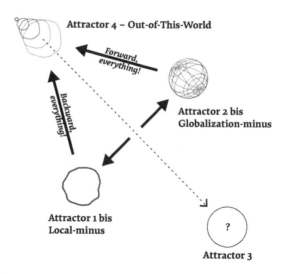

Figure 3 "Trumpism" as the political invention of a fourth attractor

to their actions. For the first time, climate change denial defines the orientation of the public life of a nation.

It is unfair to the Fascists to compare the phenomenon of which Trump is the symptom to the movements of the 1930s. The only thing the two movements have in common is that each was an invention, unforeseen within the gamut of political affects, that left the old elites totally disoriented, at least temporarily. What the Fascists had managed to put together unfolded along the old vector – the one that goes toward modernization starting from ancient cultural grounds. They managed to amalgamate the return to a dreamed-of past – Rome or Germania – with revolutionary ideals and industrial and technological modernization, while reinventing a picture of a Total State – and of a State at war – against the very idea of individual autonomy.

None of this figures in the current innovation: the State is in disgrace, the individual is king, and the urgent governmental priority is to gain time by loosening all constraints, before the population at large notices that there is no world corresponding to the America depicted.

Trump's originality is to link, in a single gesture, first the *headlong rush* toward maximum profit while abandoning the rest of the world to its fate (billionaires are called upon to represent "ordinary people"!), and second, the *headlong rush backward* of an entire people toward the return of national and ethnic categories ("Make America Great Again" behind a wall!). Instead of opposing the two movements – the advance toward globalization and the retreat toward the old national terrain – as was done earlier, Trump's supporters act as though they could be conflated. Such a fusion is obviously possible only if the very existence of the conflict between modernization, on the one hand, and the condition of being terrestrial, on the other, is denied.

Hence the constitutive role of skepticism about climate science, which is otherwise incomprehensible (let us recall that up to Clinton's presidency, Republicans and Democrats agreed on questions of political ecology[31]). We can well understand why denial prevails: the total lack of realism of the combination – Wall Street pulling millions of members of the so-called middle classes toward a return to protection of the past! – is unmistakable. For the time being, the project depends entirely on the requirement of maintaining utter indifference to the New Climatic Regime while dissolving all forms of solidarity, both external (among nations) and internal (among classes).

For the first time, a large-scale movement no longer claims to address geopolitical realities seriously, but purports to put itself explicitly outside of all worldly constraints, literally *offshore*, like a tax haven.[32] What counts above all for the elites behind this movement is no longer having to share with the others a world that they know will never again be a common world. They do all this while maintaining the American ideal of the Frontier – while taking off toward unreality! – and acting as if they wanted to get as far away as possible from the third attractor, the specter that haunts all politics and that "Trumpism" – this is its strength – has clearly detected!

(It is quite remarkable, moreover, that this invention comes from a real estate developer who has been constantly in debt, racing from failed deal to failed deal, and who became famous by way of reality television, another form of unreality and escapism.)

36

Upon promising those who were heading toward the Local-minus that they were going to rediscover the past, while also promising themselves immense profits that would stem from depriving these same voters *en masse*, the elites hardly need to quibble over empirical proofs!

It is quite useless to become outraged on the pretext that Trump voters "don't believe in facts." They are not stupid: it is because the overall geopolitical situation has to be denied that indifference to the facts becomes so essential. If the massive contradiction between advance and retreat had to be taken into account, one would have to prepare oneself to come back down to earth!

This movement defines the first government totally oriented toward the ecological question – but backwards, negatively, through rejection! This is easy to visualize if we look at figure 3, place ourselves behind Trump's back and draw a line that leads directly to where we need to go!

To be sure, "ordinary people" must not have too many illusions about what comes next in the adventure. Those for whom Trump is working are precisely those tiny elites who had grasped starting in the early 1980s that there would be no room for them and for the nine billion left behind. "Let's deregulate: let's rush to pump out bigtime everything that still remains to pump. Drill, baby, drill! We're going to win in the end, by betting on this nutcase, we'll get 30 or 40 years of respite for us and our children. After that, the deluge can come; we'll be dead by then anyway."

Accountants are quite familiar with entrepreneurs who defraud investors: the innovation of Trumpism is to have the greatest nation in the world take that step. Trump as the country's Madoff?

But we must not overlook a factor that explains the whole business: Trump presides over the country *that had the most to lose* from a return to reality. Its material infrastructures are the most difficult to reorient quickly; its responsibilities in the current climatic situation are the most crushing. Most enraging, it possesses all the scientific, technological, and organizational capabilities that could have led the "free world" to take the turn toward the third attractor.

In a sense, Trump's election confirms, for the rest of the world, the end of a politics oriented toward an identifiable goal.[33] Trumpian politics is not "post-truth," it is post-politics – that is, literally, a politics *with no object*, since it rejects the world that it claims to inhabit.

The choice is mad, but it is comprehensible. The United States saw the obstacle and, as one says of a horse that is ridden to a fence but refuses to jump, it simply refused to proceed – at least for the time being.

Given this situation, there is a chance for everyone to wake up, or so we can hope. The wall of indifference and indulgence that the climate threat alone has not managed to breach may be brought down.

Failing this, one does not need to be an anointed expert to predict that the whole business will end in a fiery deluge. This is the only real parallel with Fascism. Contrary to Marx's dictum, history does not go simply from tragedy to farce, it can repeat itself one more time in a tragic farce.

## 9.

It seems ridiculous to advance the claim that we have no more precise indications about the third attractor than the one offered by those in flight from it – as if we Moderns had never recognized the general framework of our action as well as the general direction of our history, as if we had had to wait until the end of the last century to notice that, in a way, our projects were floating in a vacuum. And yet is that not precisely the situation we are confronting? The Global (Global-plus as well as -minus) toward which we were heading up to now, the horizon that allowed us to project ourselves into an indefinite globalization (and, in reaction, the growing number of localities that were seeking to escape from this seemingly unavoidable fate), all that has never been grounded in any reality, any solid materiality.

The terrifying impression that politics has been emptied of its substance, that it is not engaged with anything at all, that it no longer has any meaning or direction, that it has become literally powerless as well as senseless, has no cause other than this gradual revelation: neither the Global nor the Local has any lasting material existence. As a result, the first vector identified above (figure 1), a straight line along which one could locate retreats and advances, resembles a freeway without any beginning or end.

If the situation is becoming clearer in spite of everything, it is because, instead of being suspended between rejection and acceptance of modernization, we now find ourselves, in a 90° shift, *suspended between the old vector and a new one*, pushed ahead by two temporal arrows that are no longer going in the same direction (figure 4). The main concern is to establish what makes up that third term. In what way can it become more *attractive* than the other two – and why does it appear so repellent to so many?

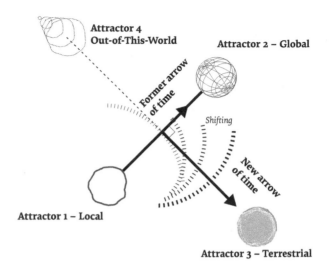

Figure 4  A reorientation of the site of politics

The first challenge is to give it a name, one that will not let it be confused with the two other attractors. "Earth"? This will be read as a reference to the planet as seen from space, the famous "Blue Planet." "Nature"? This would be much too vast. "Gaia"? This would be appropriate, but it would take pages and pages to spell out the reasons.[34] "Land"? This would be ambiguous. "World," yes, of course, but it might be too easily mixed up with the old forms of globalization.

No, we need a term that encompasses the stupefying originality (the stupefying longevity) of this agent. Let us call it, for now, the Terrestrial, with a capital T to emphasize that we are referring to a concept, and even specifying in advance where we are headed: the Terrestrial as a new *political actor*.

The massive event that we need to sum up and absorb in fact concerns the power to act of this Terrestrial, which is no longer the milieu or the background of human action. People generally talk about geopolitics as if the prefix "geo" merely designated the *framework* in which political action occurs. Yet what is changing is that, henceforth, "geo" designates an agent that participates fully in public life.

The current disorientation derives entirely from the emergence of an actor that reacts and will continue to react to human actions and that bars the modernizers from knowing *where they are*, *in what epoch*, and especially *what role* they need to play from now on.

The geopolitical strategists who pride themselves on belonging to the "realist school" will have to modify somewhat the *reality* that their battle plans are going to have to face. Formerly, it was possible to say that humans were "on earth" or "in nature," that they found themselves in "the modern period" and that they were "humans" more or less "responsible" for their actions. One could distinguish between "physical" geography and "human" geography as if it were a matter of two layers, one superimposed upon the other. But how can we say where we are if the place "on" or "in" which we are located begins to react to our actions, turns against us, encloses us, dominates us, demands something of us and carries us along in its path? How are we to distinguish from now on between physical geography and human geography?

As long as the earth seemed stable, we could speak of *space* and locate ourselves within that space and on a portion of territory that we claimed to occupy. But how are we to act if the territory itself begins to participate in history, to fight back, in short, to concern itself with us – how do we occupy a land if it is this land itself that is occupying us? The expression "I belong to a territory" has changed meaning: it now designates the agency that possesses the possessor!

If the Terrestrial is no longer the framework for human action, it is because it *participates* in that action. Space is no longer that of the cartographers, with their latitudinal and longitudinal grids. Space has become an agitated history in which we are participants among others, reacting to other reactions. It seems that we are landing in the thick of *geohistory*.[35]

To proceed toward the Global was previously to keep advancing toward an infinite horizon, to keep pushing outward a limitless frontier. If, on the contrary, one turned in the other direction, toward the Local, the hope was to recover the old security of a stable frontier and an assured identity. If it is hard to understand, today, what epoch we belong to, it is because this third attractor is at once known to everyone and completely foreign. The Terrestrial is a New World, to be sure, but it does not resemble the one the Moderns had "discovered" earlier while depopulating it in advance. It is not a new *terra incognita* for explorers in colonial headgear. It is by no means a *res nullius*, ready to be appropriated.

On the contrary, the Moderns find themselves migrating toward an earth, a land, a country, a turf, whatever one wants to call it, that is already occupied, that has been populated from time immemorial and that has more recently undergone *repopulation* by the multitude of those who have felt, well ahead of the others, the extent to which it was necessary to flee posthaste from the injunction to modernize.[36] In this world, all modern minds encounter a kind of exile. They are going to have to learn to cohabit with those whom they used to deem archaic, traditionalists, reactionaries, or simply "locals."[37]

And yet, however ancient such a space may be, it is new for everyone, since, according to the reports of climate specialists, there is quite simply *no precedent* for the current situation. Here it is, that "wicked universality," that universal lack of earth.

What is called civilization, let us say the habits acquired over the last ten millennia, has come about, the geologists explain, in an epoch and on a geographic space that have been relatively stable. The Holocene (this is what they call it) had all the features of a "framework" within which one could in fact fairly readily distinguish human actions, just as at the theater one can forget the building and the wings to concentrate on the plot.

This is no longer the case in the Anthropocene, the disputed label that some experts want to give the current epoch.[38] Here, we are no longer dealing with small fluctuations in the climate, but rather with an upheaval that is mobilizing the earth system itself.[39]

Humans have always modified their environment, of course, but the term designated only their surroundings, that which, precisely, encircled them. They remained the central figures, only modifying the decor of their dramas around the edges.

Today, the decor, the wings, the background, the whole building have come on stage and are competing with the actors for the principal role. This changes all the scripts, suggests other endings. Humans are no longer the only actors, even though they still see themselves entrusted with a role that is much too important for them.[40]

What is certain is that we can no longer tell ourselves the same old stories. Suspense prevails on all fronts.

Go backward? Relearn the old recipes? Take a new look at the age-old wisdom? Learn from the few cultures that have not yet been modernized? Yes, of course, but without lulling ourselves with illusions: for them, too, there is no precedent.

No human society, however wise, subtle, prudent, and cautious you may think it to be, has had to grapple with the reactions of the earth system to the actions of eight or nine billion humans. All the wisdom accumulated over ten thousand years, even if we were to succeed in rediscovering it, has never served more than a few hundred, a few thousand, a few million human beings on a relatively stable stage.

We understand nothing about the vacuity of contemporary politics if we do not appreciate the stunning extent to which the situation is unprecedented.

At least it is easy to understand the reaction of those who have decided to flee. How can anyone agree to turn voluntarily toward the third attractor when one was headed tranquilly toward the horizon of universal modernization?

To agree to look unblinkingly at such a situation is to position oneself like the hero of Edgar Allan Poe's short story, "Descent into the Maelstrom."[41] What distinguishes the sole survivor from the drowned victims is the cold-blooded attention with which the old sailor from the Lofoten Islands observes the movement of all the debris swirling around the vortex. When the ship is pulled into the abyss, the narrator manages to survive by attaching himself to an empty barrel.

One has to be as astute as that old sailor to believe

that escape is possible, to keep paying close attention to all the wreckage as it drifts: such attention may make it possible to understand suddenly why some of the debris is sucked toward the bottom while other objects, because of their form, can serve as life preservers. "My kingdom for a barrel!"

10.

If there is any subject that deserves lucid attention, it is that of the condition of ecology in the modern world. This territory, so ancient and so tragically new, this Terrestrial on which one would need to land, has already been crisscrossed in all directions and in all senses by what can be called the "ecological movements." These are the "green parties" that have tried to make it the new axis of public life, and who, from the beginning of the industrial revolution and especially since the post-war period, have pointed to the third attractor.

Whereas, for the Moderns, time's arrow pulled everything toward globalization, political ecology tried to tow everything toward that other pole.

We must note in all fairness that ecology succeeded so well in transforming everything into vigorous controversies – from beef to the climate, by way of hedges, humid zones, corn, pesticides, diesel fuel, urban planning, and airports – that every material object has taken on its own "ecological dimension."

Thanks to ecology, no development project fails to arouse a protest, no proposition fails to elicit an opposing one. A sign that does not deceive: the political actors who are most readily vulnerable today are the ecological militants.[42] And it is of course on the climate that the full force of the climate change deniers' rejection is focused.

Ecology has thus succeeded in running politics through its mill by introducing objects *that had not previously belonged* to the usual preoccupations of public life. It has successfully rescued politics from an overly restrictive definition of the social world. In this sense, political ecology has fully succeeded in changing what is at stake in the public sphere.

To modernize or to ecologize: this has become the crucial choice. Everyone agrees about this. And yet, ecology has failed. Everyone agrees about this too.

The Green parties remain rump parties everywhere. They never quite know what foot to put forward. When they mobilize around questions concerning "nature," the traditional parties oppose them by claiming to defend human rights. When the Green parties mobilize around "social questions," these same traditional parties ask: "What business is it of yours?"

After 50 years of Green militantism, with a few timid exceptions, people continue to oppose economics to ecology, the demands of development to those of nature, questions of social injustice to the activity of the living world.

To be fair to the ecological movements, it is expedient to situate them with respect to the three attractors in order to grasp the cause of their provisional failure. The diagnosis is fairly straightforward: the ecologists have tried to be neither on the right nor on the left, neither archaic nor progressive, without managing to get out of the trap set by the Moderns' temporal arrow.

Let us begin with the difficulty that the triangulation reveals thanks to our simple-minded schema. (It will become apparent later on why the very notion of "nature" has frozen the situation.) There are in fact at least two ways to get beyond the Right/Left division. One can take a position *in the middle* between the two extremes by settling in along the traditional vector (spine 1-2 in figure 5). But one can also redefine the vector by attaching oneself to the third attractor, which makes it necessary to redistribute the range of Left/Right positions according to another viewpoint (spines 1-3 and 2-3 in figure 5).

Numerous parties, movements, and interest groups have claimed to have discovered "a third way" between liberalism and localism, open and closed borders, cultural liberation and market economics.[43] If they have failed, up to now, it is for want of imagining a system

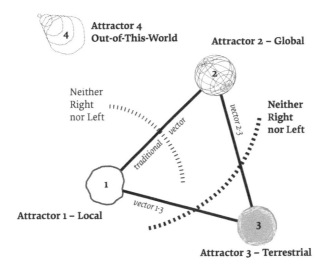

Figure 5 Two ways of locating the same slogan,
neither Right nor Left

47

of coordinates other than the one that reduced them to impotence in advance.

If it is really a question of "getting out of the Left/ Right opposition," it is not at all so that we can position ourselves *at the midpoint* of the old spine while blunting the capacity to discriminate, trim, and divide. Given the intensity of the passions that the act of calling the Left/ Right gradation into question always arouses, we must not confuse it with a new center, a new swamp, a new "soft belly."

Quite the contrary: as we see on the triangle in figure 5, it is a matter of *tilting the front line* while modifying the *content* of the disputed objects that are at the origin of the Right/Left distinction – or rather of the various Rights and Lefts, so numerous today and so intermingled that not much remains, when these labels are used, of the ordering power allowed by this classic system of coordinates.

Strangely, people claim that it is impossible to change the Left/Right vector, that it is inscribed in marble, or rather has been inscribed in the hearts of all citizens – French citizens, at least – for two centuries, even while they acknowledge that those divisions are obsolete. This proves that, for want of another vector, they persist in taking up the same old division – a repetition all the more strident in that it has less and less pertinence, like a circular saw cutting through thin air.

## 11.

Nevertheless, there must be a way to shake up this *mental hemicycle* that sets up like a row of toy soldiers first the far left, then the left, the center, the right, and finally the far right. The pattern was set in France in 1789, when elected officials fell into the habit of presenting themselves in this order before the chair of the session to vote on some obscure question involving the royal veto.

And yet, however rudimentary and contingent it may be, this gradation organizes every poll, every political proclamation, and every categorization; it is operative in every election as well as in every historical narrative, and it governs even our most visceral reactions. So much weight inheres in the terms "Right" and "Left," "conservatives" and "liberals," such floods of emotion are expressed in judgments like these: "But that guy is on the far right!" "Watch out for her: she's a leftist!"

It is hard to see, at least for the moment, how to get along without such affect-laden terms. Public action must be oriented toward a recognizable goal. However open to dispute the word "progressive" may be, it is highly unlikely that anyone can be mobilized by a call to "regress." With the "end of progress," the prospect of living less well than one's parents, the project of learning to shrivel up slowly is hardly going to electrify crowds.[44]

If the goal is to adopt a new orientation in politics, it is probably wise, in order to ensure continuity between past struggles and those to come, not to seek anything more complicated than an opposition between two terms. Nothing more complicated, but something differently oriented.

Looking at the triangle in figure 5, we see that it is possible to preserve the principle of a vector along which "reactionaries" could be distinguished from the "progressives" (if we wished to keep these labels), but

49

only if we modify the substance of the causes to be defended.

A compass, after all, is nothing but a magnetized needle and a magnetic mass. It is necessary to discover both the *angle* formed by the needle and the *composition* of the mass.

Here the hypothesis is that the needle has turned 90° and is now oriented toward the powerful attractor whose originality strikes us today, and that, despite appearances, this attractor has none of the same properties as the two others between which politics has been situated since the dawn of the so-called modern era.

The question thus becomes the following: can one preserve the principle of conflict proper to public life, while also changing its orientation?

By reorienting ourselves toward this third attractor, we shall perhaps be able to sort out the components that the Left/Right opposition had, during the modern period that is coming to an end, embraced, summed up, and contained.

The rift introduced by the Terrestrial attractor makes it necessary to open the packaging and re-examine, piece by piece, what was expected of each component – which we are gradually going to learn to call "movement," "advance," or even "progression" – and what goes clearly in the other direction – which we shall have the right henceforth to call in fact "regression," "abandonment," "betrayal," or "reaction."

This move will perhaps complicate the political game, but it will also open up unforeseen margins for maneuvering.

We can turn toward the attractor we call Terrestrial starting from the now-lapsed dream of an impossible access to the Global (the 2-3 spine in the schema), but also starting from the horizon, as far away as ever, of the return to the Local (along the spine 1-3).

The two angles allow us to identify the delicate *negotiations* that will have to be undertaken in order to *redirect* the interests of those who continue to flee toward the Global and those who continue to take refuge in the Local, in order to *interest* them in feeling the weight of this new attractor (figure 6).[45]

If we want a definition – still terribly abstract – of the new politics, we must focus on this negotiation. Allies have to be sought among people who, according to the old gradation, were clearly "reactionaries." And, of course, alliances will have to be forged with people who, again according to the old reference points, were clearly "progressives" and perhaps "liberals" or even "neoliberals."

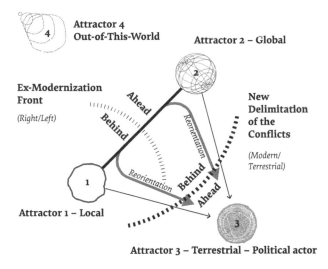

Figure 6 A new set of alliances

By what miracle could this operation of reorientation take place in a world where all the efforts to "escape from the Left/Right opposition" or "go beyond the division" or "look for a third way" have failed?

For a simple reason that is bound up with the very notion of orientation. Despite the appearances, what counts in politics are not *attitudes*, but the form and weight of the *world* to which these attitudes have the function of *reacting*.

Politics has always been oriented toward objects, stakes, situations, material entities, bodies, landscapes, places. What are called the values to be defended are always responses to the challenges of a territory that it must be possible to describe.[46] This is in effect the decisive discovery of political ecology: it is an object-oriented politics.[47] Change the territories and you will also change the attitudes.

The compass needle begins by wobbling crazily, turning in all directions, but if it ends up stabilized, it is because the magnetic mass has exercised its influence.

The only reassuring element in the current situation is that another vector is gradually gaining in realism. The Modern/Terrestrial vector (figure 6) could become a credible, perceptible, palpable alternative to the Left/Right dichotomy that remains so acute.

It is fairly easy to designate those who can appropriately be called the new adversaries: all those who continue to direct their attention toward the attractors 1, 2, and especially 4. At issue are three utopias, in the etymological sense of the word, places with no *topos*, without earth and without land: the Local, the Global, and the Out-of-This-World. But these adversaries are also the *only potential allies*. Thus, they are the ones that will have to be persuaded and converted.

First and foremost, we have to figure out how to address those who rightly feel abandoned by the historical betrayal of the ruling classes and are clamoring for the security of a protected space. In the (quite fragile) logic of the schema, it is a question of diverting toward the Terrestrial the energies that were going toward the Local attractor.

It is the uprooting that is illegitimate, not the belonging. To belong to a land, to want to stay put and keep on working one's plot of land, to be attached to it, has become "reactionary," as we have seen, only by contrast with the headlong flight forward imposed by modernization. If we stop fleeing, what does the desire for attachment look like?

The negotiation – the fraternization? – between supporters of the Local and supporters of the Terrestrial has to bear on the importance, the legitimacy, even the necessity of belonging to a land, but – and here lies the whole difficulty – without immediately confusing it with what the Local has added to it: ethnic homogeneity, a focus on patrimony, historicism, nostalgia, inauthentic authenticity.

On the contrary, there is nothing more innovative, nothing more present, subtle, technical, and artificial (in the positive sense of the word), nothing less rustic and rural, nothing more creative, nothing more contemporary than to negotiate landing on some ground.

The return to the Earth must not be confused with Lebensraum, the back-to-the-land movement promoted in France by the Vichy government during the Second World War. Movements such as Occupy Wall Street and ZAD (Zones to be Defended) in France have high-lighted the urgency of repoliticizing what it means to belong to a land.[48]

This distinction between the Local and the newly-formed land is all the more important in that the places where the different types of migrants are going to come and live have to be created from whole cloth. Whereas the Local is designed to differentiate itself by closing itself off, the Terrestrial is designed to differentiate itself by opening itself up.

And here is where the other branch of negotiation comes in, the one addressed to those who are rushing full speed ahead toward the Global. Just as the need for protection will have to be channeled toward the Terrestrial, those who are rushing toward globalization-minus will have to be shown how much that globalization differs from access to the Globe and to the world.

For the Terrestrial is bound to the earth and to land, but it is also *a way of worlding*,[49] in that it aligns with no borders, transcends all identities.

This is the sense in which it solves the problem of place we noted earlier: there is no Earth corresponding to the infinite horizon of the Global, but at the same time the Local is much too narrow, too shrunken, to accommodate the multiplicity of beings belonging to the terrestrial world. This is why the zoom lens that purported to align the Local and the Global as successive sightings along a single trajectory has never made any sense.

Whatever alliances have to be woven, it is certain that we shall be incapable of achieving them as long as we continue to speak of political attitudes, affects, passions, and positions while the real world toward which those attitudes, affects, passions, and positions are directed has completely changed.

In other words, we have *fallen behind* in revamping our political affects. This is why we need to restart the process and put the new magnetic mass in front of the traditional compass: to discover the direction it will indicate and see how our attitudes, affects, passions, and positions will turn out to be redistributed.

There is no point hiding the difficulties from ourselves: the fight is going to be a hard one. The time lost in continuing to pace up and down along the old Right/ Left vector has delayed the necessary mobilizations and negotiations.

This is indeed what has slowed the rise of the ecological parties: they have sought to situate themselves between the Right and the Left or to "transcend" the Right/Left cleavage, but without ever specifying the *place* from which one could imagine such a transcendence. Having failed to take a step sideways, they have found themselves squeezed between the two attractors, which for their part have been gradually emptied of all reality. It is hardly astonishing that the parties, too, are going nowhere fast.

Are we not beginning to discern, more clearly every day, the premises of a new affect that would reorient the forces at work in a lasting way? Are we not beginning to ask ourselves: *Are we Moderns or Terrestrials?*

Political scientists will say that one never invents a new orientation in relation to such fundamental values as those that run from Left to Right; to which historians will perhaps retort: "Were there people 'on the right' and people 'on the left' before the eighteenth century?"

What is important is to be able to get out of the

impasse by imagining a set of new alliances: "You have never been a leftist? That doesn't matter, neither have I, but, like you, I am *radically Terrestrial!*" A whole set of positions that we shall have to learn to recognize, before the militants of the extreme Modern have totally devastated the stage.

12.

The proof that ecology as a movement has not succeeded in defining that consummate political actor, the Terrestrial, with enough precision is that ecology has not known how to mobilize on a scale adequate to the stakes. It is always surprising to see how much distance there is between the power of the emotions aroused by social questions since the nineteenth century and the power of the ecological movements since the post-war period.

One good indicator of the distance is Karl Polanyi's admirable book *The Great Transformation*. What is heartbreaking, when one reads Polanyi, is obviously not that he was mistaken in thinking that the ravages of free-market liberalism were behind him, it is that these ravages have elicited only a response that could be called *the great immobility* of the political geography. His book dates from 1945; the ensuing decades have marked out with precision the place, alas empty, of the other *great transformation* that should have occurred, if only the ecological movements had taken up, prolonged, and intensified the energy created by the various types of socialism.

But that transmission has never really taken place. Having failed to figure out how to join forces effectively, socialism and ecology, each of which sought to alter the course of history, have only managed to slow it down. If they have been too weak, it is because they believed they faced a choice between focusing on social questions or focusing on ecological questions, when what was really at stake was a different and much more decisive choice having to do with *two directions* of politics: one that defines social questions in a restrictive manner, and another that defines the stakes of survival without introducing *a priori* differences between humans and non-humans. The choice to be made is between a narrow definition of the social ties making up a society, and a wider definition of associations that make up what have been called collectives.[50]

These two directions do not target different actors. To resort to a cliché, we don't have to choose between workers' wages and the fate of some little birds, but between two types of worlds in which there are *both* workers' salaries and little birds, but associated differently in the two contexts.

The question then becomes the following: why did the social movements not grasp the ecological stakes at the outset *as if they were their own*, which would have allowed them to avoid obsolescence and to lend their strength to a still-weak ecology? Or, to turn the question around, why did political ecology *fail to take up the baton from the social question* and forge ahead?

During the 70 years that specialists call the "Great Acceleration,"[51] everything has changed – the market forces have been unleashed, the reaction of the earth system has been triggered – yet progressive and reactionary politics still continue to be defined along the sole sempiternal vector, that of modernization and emancipation.

57

On the one hand, major transformations; on the other, almost total immobility in the definition, positioning, and aspirations associated with the word "socialism." Along the same lines, we can point to the immense difficulties encountered by feminists as they have sought to bring to the forefront their own battles, long deemed "peripheral" in relation to the struggles for social transformation. It is as though the compass were stuck.[52]

Instead of merging these revolts, we have only managed to submit, in almost total impotence, to the Great Acceleration, the defeat of communism, the triumph of globalization-minus, the sterilization of socialism, only to end up with the latest circus, the election of Donald Trump! Before other catastrophes that we shudder to anticipate.

During all these events, we have been stuck with a scarcely attenuated opposition between "social" conflicts and "ecological" conflicts – as if we were dealing with two distinct entities between which, like Buridan's legendary ass, we have to continue to hesitate while dying of hunger and thirst. But nature is no more a sack of grain than society is a bucket of water. If there is no choice to be made, it is for the excellent reason that there are not naked humans on one side and nonhuman objects on the other.

Ecology is not the name of a party, or even of something to worry about; it is a call for a change of direction: "Toward the Terrestrial!"


## 13.

How can this interruption in relaying a collective struggle be explained?

The old grid that allowed us to distinguish "progressives" from "reactionaries" was defined, starting with the emergence of "the social question" in the nineteenth century, by notions of *social classes*, notions that depended in turn on the specific positions these classes occupied in what was called "the process of production."

Despite all the efforts to attenuate class oppositions and even to claim that they no longer made any sense, politics was nevertheless organized around them.

The effectiveness of interpretations of public life in terms of class struggle derived from the seemingly material, concrete, empirical character of the opposing categories. Thus, these interpretations were called "materialist," and they were generally undergirded by what was called economics.

All the revisions notwithstanding, this type of interpretation was widely adopted and maintained throughout the twentieth century. Even today, it is used to identify those who are "moving ahead" and those who are "betraying the forces of progress" (even if, once again, attitudes diverge depending on whether moral standards or economic issues are in question). On the whole, we have remained Marxist.

If these definitions have begun to spin their wheels in a vacuum, it is because the analysis in terms of social classes and the materialism underlying that analysis were clearly defined by the attractor called Global, above, in opposition with the Local.

The great phenomena of industrialization, urbanization, and occupation of colonized territories defined a horizon – sinister or radiant, it hardly matters – that gave meaning and direction to progress. And for a good reason: that progress was pulling out of poverty, if not out of exploitation, hundreds of millions of human beings whose contrivances were supposed to lead toward an emancipation that seemed inevitable.

Despite their constant misunderstandings, Rightists and Leftists kept on competing to see who would be the more resolutely modernizing, which side would reach the Global world first, squabbling all the while over whether they should proceed through reform or through revolution. But they never took the time to explain to peoples undergoing modernization *what* precisely described *world* progress would end up putting them in.

What they did not foresee (but what they might perfectly well have foreseen!)[53] was that this horizon of progress would be transformed little by little into a mere *horizon*, a simple regulating idea, a sort of increasingly vague utopia, as the gradually evolving Earth would fail to give it substance.

Until the event of December 13, 2015, mentioned at the beginning of this essay, the conclusion of COP21, made it official, as it were, that there was no longer an Earth corresponding to the horizon of the Global.

If the analyses in terms of class have never allowed the Leftists to stand up to their enemies in a lasting way (which explains why Polanyi's predictions about the extinction of liberalism were wrong), it is because their definition of the material world was so abstract, so ideal, not to say so idealistic, that they never had a firm grip on this new reality.

To be a materialist, one has to have matter; to give a worldly definition of activity, one has to meet a world; to occupy a territory, one has to live on Earth; to take up *Realpolitik*, one has to be a realist.

Yet throughout the entire twentieth century, even though analyses and experiments based on a classic definition of the class struggle were developing, a metamorphosis of the very definition of matter, of the world, of the Earth on which everything rested, was taking place more or less surreptitiously, in any case without much notice being taken by the Left.

The question thus becomes how to define class struggles much more realistically by taking into account this new materiality, the new materialism imposed by the orientation toward the Terrestrial.[54]

Polanyi overestimated society's ability to resist marketization because he was counting on support from human actors alone and on their awareness of the limits of merchandise and of the market. However, these actors are no longer the only ones to revolt. Polanyi could not have anticipated the *addition* of powerful forces of resistance thrust into the class conflicts and capable of transforming their stakes. The outcome of the disputes can only be modified if all rebels, in overlapping configurations, are entrusted with the task of fighting.

If the so-called social classes were identified earlier by their place in the system of production, we see now that that system was defined much too narrowly.

Analysts of course had long since added to the strict definition of social classes a whole apparatus of values, cultures, attitudes, and symbols to refine their definitions and explain why the groups did not always pursue their "objective interests." And yet, even if "class cultures" are added to "class interests," these groups do not have territories around them that are populated enough for them to be able to connect integrally with reality and become self-aware. Their definition remains social, excessively social.[55]

Below the class struggles, other ways to classify. Below the "last instance," yet another instance. Below matter, more matters.

Timothy Mitchell has shown, for example, that economies based on coal over time allowed a persistent class struggle that the shift to oil has permitted the ruling classes to win,[56] even though social classes, as traditionally defined, had remained the same, with workers being defended by unions.

Yes, but *territorially defined* classes cannot be stratified in the same way. The opportunity for miners to block production, organize deep down in the mines away from their supervisors, form alliances with the railroad workers operating near their slag heaps, send their wives to demonstrate under the windows of their boss, all that disappears with oil controlled by a few expatriate engineers in distant countries led by tiny and easily corruptible elites, and whose product circulates through quickly-repaired pipelines. Visible with coal, the enemies have become invisible with oil.

Mitchell is not content to emphasize the "spatial dimension" of the workers' struggles; that would be a truism. He draws attention to the very composition of what the bond with coal or with oil does to the earth, the workers, the engineers, and the companies.[57] Moreover, he draws a paradoxical consequence: from the post-war period on, thanks to oil, nations have been entering the reign of an Economy that believes it can do without any material limits!

For class struggles depend on a *geo-logic*.

The introduction of the prefix "geo-" does not make

150 years of Marxist or materialist analysis obsolete; on the contrary, it obliges us to *reopen the social question* while *intensifying* it through the new geopolitics.[58]

Since the map of the struggles of *social classes* gives us less and less of a hold on political life – analysts have been reduced to complaining that people "no longer follow their own class interests" – we shall have to draw maps of the *struggles of geo-social loci* in order to identify at last what the real interests of these loci are, with whom they are going to make alliances, and against whom they are going to fight.[59]

The nineteenth century was the age of the social question; the twenty-first is the age of the *new geo-social question*.

If they don't manage to change maps, the parties on the Left will look like bushes after a plague of locusts: nothing will be left but a cloud of dusty remains good only for burning.

The difficulty is that to find principles that will allow us to define these new classes and trace the lines of conflict between their divergent interests, we shall have to learn to distrust definitions of matter, the system of production, and even the reference points in space and time that had served to define ecological struggles as well as social classes.

In fact, one of the oddities of the modern period is that we have had a definition of matter that is hardly material, hardly terrestrial at all. The Moderns take pride in a realism that they have never been able to put to work. How can one qualify as materialists people who are capable of inadvertently letting the temperature of their planet rise by 3.5°C on average, or who inflict on their fellow citizens the role of

63

agents of the sixth extinction without anyone even noticing?

This may seem strange, but when the Moderns talk about politics, one never knows in what practical framework they are situating its enactment.

In sum, "the concrete analysis of the concrete situation," as Lenin used to say, is never concrete enough. Ecology has always said to the socialists: "Try a little harder, you materialist ladies and gentlemen, to be materialists at last!"

## 14.

If amalgamating – as in the context of wars of revolution – the old veterans of the class struggle and the new recruits to the geo-social conflicts has not been possible, the fault lies in the role that both groups have attributed to "nature." Here is one of those cases in which, literally, ideas lead the world.

A certain conception of "nature" has allowed the Moderns to occupy the Earth in such a way that it forbids others to occupy their own territories differently. For, in order to mold a politics, you need *agents* who bring together their interests and their capacities for action. But you cannot make alliances between political actors and *objects* that are external to society and deprived of the power to act. This dilemma is very well expressed by the French Zadists when they write: "We are not defending nature, we are nature defending itself."[60]

For the exteriority attributed to objects is not a given encountered through experience, but the result of a quite particular political-scientific history that we need

64

to examine briefly in order to restore more leeway to politics.

It is obvious that the question of the sciences is central if we are to survey the Terrestrial. Without the sciences, what would we know of the New Climatic Regime? And how could we forget that sciences have become the privileged target of the climate change deniers?

But we still need to know how to grasp them. If we swallow the usual epistemology whole, we shall find ourselves again prisoners of a conception of "nature" that is impossible to politicize since it has been invented precisely to limit human action thanks to an appeal to the laws of objective nature that cannot be questioned. Freedom on one side, strict necessity on the other: this makes it possible to have it both ways.[61] Every time we want to count on the power to act of other actors, we're going to encounter the same objection: "Don't even think about it, these are mere objects, they cannot react," the way Descartes said of animals that they cannot suffer.

However, if we claim to be opposing "scientific rationality" by inventing a more intimate, more subjective, more rooted, more global – more "ecological," as it were – way of capturing our ties to "nature," we lose on both fronts: we will be left with the idea of "nature" borrowed from tradition while being deprived of the contribution of positive knowledge.

We need to be able to count on *the full power of the sciences*, but *without the ideology of "nature"* that has been attached to that power. We have to be materialist and rational, but we have to shift these qualities onto the right grounds.

The difficulty is that the Terrestrial is not at all the

Globe. One cannot be materialist and rational in the same way in these two sites.

In the first place, it is clear that one cannot praise rationality without recognizing to what extent it has been abused by the quest for the Global.

How could we deem "realistic" a project of modernization that has "forgotten" for two centuries to anticipate the reactions of the terraqueous globe to human actions? How could we accept as "objective" economic theories that are incapable of integrating into their calculations the scarcity of resources whose exhaustion it had been their mission to predict?[62] How could we speak of "effectiveness" with respect to technological systems that have not managed to integrate into their design a way to last more than a few decades? How could we call "rationalist" an ideal of civilization guilty of a forecasting error so massive that it prevents parents from leaving an inhabited world to their children?[63]

It is hardly astonishing that the word rationality has become somewhat frightening. Before accusing ordinary people of attaching no value to the facts of which so-called rational people want to convince them, let us recall that, if they have lost all common sense, it is because they have been masterfully betrayed.

To restore a positive meaning to the words "realistic," "objective," "efficient," or "rational," we have to turn them away from the Global, where they have so clearly failed, and toward the Terrestrial.

How can this difference in orientation be defined? The two poles are almost the same, except that the Globe grasps all things from *far away*, as if they were *external* to the social world and completely *indifferent* to human concerns. The Terrestrial grasps the same structures from *up close*, as *internal* to the collectivities and *sensitive* to human actions, to which they *react* swiftly. Two very different versions of the way for these very scientists to have their feet on the ground, as it were.

This is a new *libido sciendi*, a new distribution of the metaphors and sensitivities that are essential to the recovery and reorientation of political affects.

The Global has to be viewed as a *declension* of the Globe that has ended up distorting access to it. So just what has happened?

The idea – the revolutionary idea – of grasping the earth as one planet among others, immersed in an infinite universe of essentially similar bodies, can be traced to the birth of the modern sciences. To simplify, this has been called the invention of *Galilean objects*.[64]

The progress of this planetary vision has been enormous. It defines the cartographer's globe, the globe of the earliest earth sciences. It makes physics possible.

Unfortunately, it is also very easy to distort. From the fact that one can, *from the vantage point of the earth*, grasp the planet as a falling body among other falling bodies in the infinite universe, some thinkers go on to conclude that it is necessary to occupy, virtually, *the vantage point of the universe* to understand what is happening on this planet.

The fact that one can gain access to remote sites *from the earth* becomes the *duty* to gain access to the earth *from remote sites*.

Such a conclusion is in no way obligatory. In practice, it will always remain a contradiction in terms: the offices, universities, laboratories, instruments, academies, in short, the entire circuit of production and validation of knowledge *has never left* the old terrestrial soil.[65] No matter how far out they send their thoughts, researchers always have their feet firmly anchored in clay.

And yet this vision from the vantage point of the universe – "the view from nowhere" – has become the new common sense to which the terms "rational" and even "scientific" find themselves durably attached.[66]

From now on, it is from this Great Outside that the old primordial Earth is going to be known, weighed, and judged. What was only a virtuality is becoming, for the greatest minds as well as the smallest, an exciting project: *to know is to know from the outside.* Everything has to be viewed as if from Sirius – a Sirius of the imagination, to which no one has ever had access.

Furthermore, this promotion of the Earth as a planet that has become part of the infinite universe, a body among bodies, has the disadvantage of limiting to just a few movements – at the beginning of the scientific revolution, to just one: the falling of bodies – the whole gamut of movements grasped by the positive sciences.[67]

Yet on the Earth seen from the inside, there are many other forms of movements that have become harder and harder to take into account. Little by little, it has become more cumbersome to gain objective knowledge about a whole range of *transformations*: genesis, birth, growth, life, death, decay, metamorphoses.

The detour by way of the outside introduced into the notion of "nature" a confusion from which we have still not been extricated.

Until the sixteenth century, this concept could include a whole gamut of movements – this is the etymological sense of the Latin *natura* or the Greek *phusis*, which could be translated as origin, engendering, process, the course of things; now, the word "natural" is increasingly reserved for what makes it possible to follow a single type of movement viewed from the outside. This is the meaning that the word has taken on in the expression "the natural sciences."

This would not be a problem if the term had been restricted to the sciences of the universe, that is, to the infinite spaces known *from the vantage point of the earth's surface* through the exclusive intermediary of instruments and calculations. But there has been a push to go further, a desire to know in the very same way everything that happens on earth as if one had to see it from afar.

Whereas we had before our eyes a range of phenomena demanding nothing more than to be grasped by positive sciences, many scientists deliberately distanced themselves from them to the extent that, by a sort of sadistic asceticism, they began to discern in all these easily accessible movements *only those* that one *could have seen* from Sirius.

Every movement had to conform to the model of falling bodies. This is called the "mechanistic" view of the world, thanks to a strange metaphor borrowed from an inaccurate idea about the working of real mechanisms.[68]

All other movements have become subject to suspicion. Considered from the inside, on the Earth, they could not be scientific; they could not be really naturalized.

Hence the classic division between *knowledge* seen from afar but assured, and *imagination*, which saw things up close but without grounding in reality: at worst, simple fairy tales; at best, ancient myths, respectable but without verifiable content.

If the planet has ended up moving away from the Terrestrial, it is because everything has happened as though nature seen from the universe had begun to *replace*, bit by bit – to cover over, to chase away – nature seen from the Earth, the nature that grasped, that could have grasped, that should have continued to include, all the phenomena of genesis.

The grandiose Galilean invention has come to take up all the space by making people forget that seeing the earth from Sirius is only a tiny part – even if the infinite universe is involved – of what we have the right to know positively.

The inevitable consequence: we have begun to see less and less of what is happening on Earth.

Necessarily, from Sirius we risk missing a lot of events, while developing a lot of illusions about the rationality or irrationality of Planet Earth!

If we recall all the bizarre things that earthbound beings, over the last three or four centuries, have imagined they discerned on the red planet before noticing their errors, we shall not be surprised by all the errors committed, over the last three or four centuries, regarding the fate of the terrestrial civilizations as seen from Sirius!

The ideals of rationality, like the accusations of irrationality brought against the Earth and the earthbound? So many pipe dreams, so many moons made of green cheese, so many canals on Mars ...

## 15.

Such a bifurcation between the real – external, objective, and knowable – and the inside – unreal, subjective,

70

and unknowable – would have intimidated no one, or would have been taken for a simple exaggeration on the part of savants not very well acquainted with the realities here below, had it not been *superimposed* on the notorious vector of modernization identified earlier.[69]

It is on this point that the two meanings, positive and negative, of the word "Global" turn out to diverge entirely.

The subjective side begins to be associated with the archaic and the outdated; the objective side with the modern and the progressive. Seeing things from the inside comes to have no value other than being traditional, intimate, archaic. Seeing things from the outside, on the contrary, becomes the only way to grasp the reality that counts, and, above all, the only way to orient oneself toward the *future*.

It is this brutal division that was to give consistency, as it were, to the illusion of the Global as the horizon of modernity. From this point on it was necessary, even if one stayed in place, to shift one's position virtually, bag and baggage, away from subjective and sensitive positions toward exclusively objective positions, finally freed of all sensitivity – or rather of sentimentality.

This is where, by contrast with the Global, the necessarily reactive, reflexive, nostalgic figure of the Local comes in (see figure 1).

Losing one's sensitivity to nature as process – according to the old sense of the term "nature" – was becoming the only way to gain access to nature as an infinite universe – according to the new definition. To progress in modernity was to tear oneself away from the primordial soil and set out for the Great Outside, to become if not natural, as least *naturalist*.[70]

Through a strange perversion of metaphors of giving birth, *no longer depending* on those old forms of genesis was what would allow us to "be born at last to modernity."

As feminists have shown by analyzing witchcraft trials, hatred of a large number of values traditionally associated with women would come from this tragic metamorphosis, rendering grotesque all forms of attachment to the old soils.[71] The effort to resist the attraction to any form of grounding was a way of saying – as the hypocrite priest Tartuffe said to his host's daughter – "Cover that bosom, girl." From then on, objectivity became gendered.

This great displacement – the only real "Great Replacement"[72] – will then be imposed on the entire world, which becomes the landscape of globalization-minus as the last vestiges of adherence to the old nature-as-process are durably eradicated.

This is the meaning of the expression that is now out of fashion, but whose echoes are still heard whenever anyone speaks of progress, development, and the future: "We are going to modernize the planet, which is in the process of unification."

Either one speaks of "nature," but then one is far away; or else one is close by, but one expresses only feelings. Such is the result of the confusion between the planetary vision and the Terrestrial. It is about the planetary vision that one can say, considering things "from above," that it has always varied and that it will outlast humans, making it possible to take the New Climatic Regime as an unimportant oscillation. The Terrestrial, for its part, does not allow this kind of detachment.[73]

Thus, it is easy to understand why it is impossible to offer a very precise description of conflicts over attachment to land and why one must learn to demystify the notion of "nature," which purports to encompass these two attractors.

When the so-called "ecological" parties try to interest people in what is happening "to nature," a nature that they claim to be "protecting," if by the term "nature" is meant the nature-universe seen from nowhere that is supposed to stretch from the cells of our bodies to the most distant galaxies, the answer will be simply: "That's too far away; it's too vague; it doesn't concern us; we couldn't care less."

And the speaker will be right. No progress will be made toward a "politics of nature" as long as the same term is used to designate, for example, research into terrestrial magnetism, the classification of the 3,500 exoplanets that have been spotted to date, the detection of gravitational waves, the role of earthworms in soil aeration, the reaction of shepherds in the Pyrenees to the reintroduction of bears, or the reaction of bacteria in our intestines to our latest gastronomic overindulgence. That nature is a real catch-all.

There is no point looking any further for the slow pace of mobilizations in favor of nature-as-universe. It is completely incapable of churning anything political. To make that type of beings – the Galilean objects – the model for what is going to mobilize us in geo-social conflicts is to court failure. Trying to mobilize that nature in class conflicts is like getting ready to go out on a protest march by stepping into concrete.

In order to begin to describe objectively, rationally, effectively, in order to paint the terrestrial situation with some degree of realism, we need all the sciences, but *positioned differently*.

In other words, to be knowledgeable in scientific terms, it does not help to be beamed up to Sirius. It is not necessary, either, to shun rationality in order to add feelings to cold knowledge. It is essential to acquire as much cold-blooded knowledge as possible about the *heated* activity *of an Earth* finally grasped *from up close*.

## 16.

It all depends, obviously, on what one means by "heated activity." It is easy to understand that, seen from the vantage point of the nature-universe, the earth's agency looks like a subjective illusion, like a simple projection of feelings onto an indifferent "nature."

Thus, as early as the seventeenth century, when economists began to take "nature" into account, they took it as a mere "factor in production," a resource that was precisely *external, indifferent to our actions*, grasped from *afar, as if by foreigners* pursuing goals that were *indifferent* to the Earth.

In what we call *systems of production*, it was known how to identify human agents – workers, capitalists – as well as artificial infrastructures – machines, factories, cities, agrobusiness – but it was impossible to take the beings that had in the meantime become "natural" (seen from Sirius) as agents, actors, animated, acting entities of the same caliber.

It was vaguely felt that everything else *depended* on them and that they were inevitably going to *react*, but – here's the hitch – because nature-as-universe had so fully obscured nature-as-process, those who were seizing control of these resources, sometimes fearfully, were left devoid of words, concepts, and directions.

One could of course go rummaging in the archives of other peoples to discover attitudes, myths, and rituals that were absolutely untouched by any notion of "resource" or "production," but these findings were taken, at the time, as mere vestiges of old forms of subjectivity, of archaic cultures irreversibly outstripped by the modernization front.[74] The testimony was moving, to be sure, but appropriate for ethnographic museums.

It is only today that all these practices have become precious models for learning how to survive in the future.[75]

The relation to the sciences can change only if, among the so-called natural sciences, those that focus on nature-as-process (*natura* or *phusis*) are carefully distinguished from those that focus on the universe. Whereas the latter start with the planet taken as a body among bodies, for the former the Earth appears wholly singular.

For an excellent illustration of the contrast, let us compare a world made up of *Galilean objects* with that same world composed of *agents* that could be called Lovelockian, in honor of James Lovelock (the name is used here, like Galileo's, to summarize a much longer line of scholars[76]).

For those who adhere to the sciences of nature-as-universe, there has been a major misunderstanding of the argument of biochemists such as Lovelock, according to whom it is necessary to consider, on Earth, living beings as agents participating fully in the processes of generating the chemical, and even in part the geological, conditions of the planet.[77]

75

If the composition of the air we breathe depends on living beings, the atmosphere is no longer simply the environment in which living beings are located and in which they evolve; it is, in part, a result of their actions. In other words, there are not organisms on one side and an environment on the other, but a coproduction by both. *Agencies* are redistributed.

The difficulty we have understanding the role of living beings – their power to act, their agency – in the evolution of terrestrial phenomena reproduces the difficulty of understanding the phenomenon of life in earlier periods. Not to mention the difficulty of interpreting human actions as seen from Sirius.

In fact, if we take the model of falling bodies as the yardstick for movement in general, all the other movements, agitations, transformations, initiatives, combinations, metamorphoses, processes, entanglements, and overlaps are going to appear bizarre. To grasp them, many more epicycles than the ancient astronomers had to invent to capture the movement of the planets would have to be imagined.

The simplification introduced by Lovelock in the comprehension of terrestrial phenomena is not at all that he added "life" to the Earth, or that he made the Earth a "living organism," but, quite to the contrary, that he *stopped denying* that living beings were active participants in biochemical and geochemical phenomena. His reductionist argument is the exact opposite of vitalism. He refuses to *de-animate* the planet by *removing most of the actors* that intervene all along a causal chain.[78] No more and no less than this.

While there is no need to adopt Lovelock's approach as such, it is important to grasp the political reorientation that would be possible if we were to conceive of the natural sciences as encompassing all the activities necessary to our existence.

The physical laws are the same on Sirius and on the Earth, but they do not produce the same results.

With Galilean objects as the model, we can indeed take nature as a "resource to exploit," but with Lovelockian agents, it is useless to nurture illusions. Lovelock's objects have agency, they are going to react – first chemically, biochemically, geologically – and it would be naïve to believe that they are going to remain inert no matter how much pressure is put on them.

In other words, economists may make nature a factor in production, but this would not occur to someone who has read Lovelock – or Humboldt, for that matter.[79]

The conflict can be summarized simply: there are those who continue to look at things from the vantage point of Sirius and simply do not see that the earth system reacts to human action, or do not believe it possible; they still hope that the Earth will mysteriously be beamed to Sirius and become one planet among others.[80] Basically, they do not believe that there is *life* on Earth capable of suffering and reacting. And there are those who seek, while keeping a firm grip on the sciences, to understand what is meant by distributing action, animation, the power to act, all along the causal chains in which they find themselves entangled. The former are climate skeptics (through a taste for distance if not through active corruption); the latter consent to *face up to* an enigma *concerning the number and nature of the agents at work.*

77

## 17

To move ahead in the effort to describe the geo-social conflicts, it is clear that we cannot do without science and reason, but also that we must both broaden and *limit* the reach of the empirical sciences. These sciences must be extended to encompass all processes of genesis, in order to avoid imposing a priori restrictions on the agency of the beings with which we shall have to work. Yet the empirical sciences must also be subjected to certain limits.

In particular, it is important to try to single out the sciences that bear upon what some researchers call the *Critical Zone(s)*.[81]

Seen from space, everything that has to do with knowledge of the third attractor, the Terrestrial, is in fact limited in a surprising way to a minuscule zone a few kilometers thick between the atmosphere and bedrock. A biofilm, a varnish, a skin, a few infinitely folded layers.

Speak of nature in general as much as you like, wonder at the immensity of the universe, dive down in thought to the boiling center of the planet, gasp in fear before those infinite spaces, this will not change the fact that everything that concerns you resides in the minuscule Critical Zone. This is the point of departure and also the point of return for all the sciences that matter to us.

This is why we need to circumscribe, among the fields of positive knowledge, those that have to do with the Critical Zone, so that we will not have to weigh ourselves down with the entire universe every time we talk about territorial conflicts.

In political philosophy, there is another good reason for holding to such a distinction. Although the sciences of nature-as-universe are certainly attached to the Earth, they deal with far-away phenomena that can be known only through the intermediary of instruments, models, and calculations. It does not make a lot of sense, at least for ordinary mortals, to claim to offer alternatives or to challenge the quality of this research. In the face of their results, we all find ourselves in the normal situation of learning what experts have to say about them – while retaining the right not to be interested.

The situation is entirely different for the sciences of nature-as-process that bear upon the Critical Zone. Here, researchers find themselves confronting competing bodies of knowledge that they never have the power to disqualify a priori.[82] They have to confront conflicts for each of the agents that populate the zone and that have neither the privilege nor the possibility of remaining uninterested.

Few people will campaign for an alternative vision of black holes or magnetic inversion, but we know from experience that about soils, vaccines, earthworms, bears, wolves, neurotransmitters, mushrooms, water circulation, or the composition of air, the smallest study will immediately be plunged into a full-scale battle of interpretations. The Critical Zone is not a classroom; the relationship between researchers and the public is anything but purely pedagogical.

If we still had any doubts on this point, the pseudo-controversy over the climate suffices to dispel them.[83] There is no evidence that any major corporation has spent a penny to produce ignorance about the detection of the Higgs boson. But denying the climatic mutation is another matter entirely: financing floods in. Ignorance on the part of the public is such a precious commodity that it justifies immense investments.[84]

In other words, the sciences of nature-as-process cannot have the same somewhat lofty and disinterested epistemology as that of the sciences of nature-as-universe. The philosophy that protected the latter will be of no help to the former. With no hope of escaping the controversies, the sciences of nature-as-process would do better to organize themselves in order to resist all those that do take an interest – a great interest – in them.

The essential political point is that the Earth's reaction to human action looks like an aberration in the eyes of those who believe in a terrestrial world made up of Galilean objects, and it appears self-evident to those who see it as a concatenation of Lovelockian agents.

If we accept what precedes, we understand that the third attractor does not have much to do with "nature" – in the sense of nature-as-universe – as it used to be imagined, either as Globe or as Global.

It is through the Terrestrial that we must henceforth understand the conjoined action of the agents known through the sciences of the Critical Zone, which are struggling for legitimacy and autonomy against countless other concerned parties that have contradictory interests, and all of which possess other bodies of positive knowledge. The Terrestrial is literally drawing another world, as different from "nature" as from what used to be called the "human world" or "society." The three are all political entities, but they do not lead to the same occupation of the soil, to the same "land-grabbing."

One can also understand that discovering this new world requires different psychological equipment, a *libido sciendi* different from the one needed for setting off toward the Global. Targeting emancipation through weightlessness does not require the same virtues as targeting emancipation through a process of plowing, a way to dig in. Innovating by breaking all limits and all codes is not the same as innovating by profiting from these limits. Celebrating the forward march of progress cannot have the same meaning when one is heading toward the Global as it does when one is heading toward "decisive advances" in taking the Earth's reactions to our actions into account.

In both cases, it is a matter of positive bodies of knowledge, and yet these do not involve the same scientific adventures, the same laboratories, the same instruments, the same investigations, nor are the same researchers heading toward each of these two attractors.

The strategic advantage of such a distinction is to ensure a certain continuity with the spirit of innovation, enterprise, and discovery, which seems indispensable if we wish to avoid driving the aforementioned Moderns, who are also potential allies, to despair. The spirit of innovation remains, but it is applied to different issues.

The period opening up before us is indeed a new epoch of "great discoveries," but these resemble neither the wholesale conquest of a New World emptied of its inhabitants, as before, nor the headlong flight into a form of hyper-neo-modernity; instead, they require digging deep down into the Earth with its thousand folds.

An Earth – we learn this quickly with a mix of enthusiasm and fright – that has more than one trick in its bag and that is insinuating itself as a third party in all our actions. In both cases it is a matter – to hold onto one of the mainsprings of the modern tradition – of *moving beyond*, but by violating different taboos, by passing through different Pillars of Hercules.

18.

Redirecting attention from "nature" toward the Terrestrial might put an end to the disconnect that has frozen political positions since the appearance of the climate threat and has imperiled the linking of the so-called social struggles with those we call ecological.

The new articulation between the two struggles correlates with a shift from an analysis focused on a *system of production* to an analysis focused on a *system of engendering*. The two analyses differ first of all in their principles – freedom for the first, dependency for the second. They differ next in the role given to humanity – central for the first, distributed for the second. Finally, they differ in the type of movements for which they take responsibility – mechanism for the first, genesis for the second.

The system of production was based on a certain conception of nature, materialism, and the role of the sciences; it assigned a different function to politics and was rooted in a division between human actors and their resources. At bottom, there was the idea that human freedom would be deployed in a natural setting where it would be possible to indicate the precise limits of each property.

The system of engendering brings into confrontation agents, actors, animate beings that all have distinct capacities for reacting. It does not proceed from the

82

same conception of materiality as the system of production, it does not have the same epistemology, and it does not lead to the same form of politics. It is not interested in producing goods, for humans, on the basis of resources, *but in engendering* terrestrials – not just humans, but all terrestrials. It is based on the idea of cultivating attachments, operations that are all the more difficult because animate beings are not limited by frontiers and are constantly overlapping, embedding themselves within one another.

If these two systems enter into conflict, it is because another authority has appeared, making it necessary to raise all the old questions again, no longer starting from the project of emancipation alone, but starting from the newly rediscovered value of dependency.

Dependency comes in first of all to limit, then to complicate, then to reconsider the project of emancipation, in order finally to amplify it. As if, through a new dialectical pirouette, one were inverting the Hegelian project once again.[85] As if the Spirit had never finished being reincarnated.

It is this new form of obligation that is emphasized in the assertion that there is no planet (one should say Critical Zone) that can shelter the utopia of modernization or of globalization-minus. How can we deny that we find ourselves facing *another power* that imposes barriers different from the old so-called "natural" limits?[86]

It is this same conflict of authority that the obscurantist elites had identified perfectly when they decided no longer to share the planet with the rest of the nine billion good folks whose fate – at least so they claimed – had always been their chief concern. Are they not unveiling the new *authority* from which they seek to conceal their misdoings?[87]

It is this same contradiction that broke out in diplomatic form on December 12, 2015, at the conclusion of the Paris Climate Accord, when every delegation muttered to itself: "But then there is no world for all our development projects?!"

What power then secured the signature of those 175 states, if not a form of sovereignty to which they consented to bow down and that propelled them to reach agreement? If it is not a *power* that *dominates* the heads of state, and to which they grant a still-vague form of *legitimacy*, what should it be called?

It is this same contradiction that the term Anthropocene sums up, however disputed its date of origin and its definition may be: "The earth system reacts henceforth to your action in such a way that you no longer have a stable and indifferent framework in which to lodge your desires for modernization." Despite all the criticisms to which the concept has been subjected, the prefix "Anthropos" applied to a geological period is indeed the symptom of a repoliticization of all the planetary questions. As if a label "Made by Humans" had been engraved on all the old natural resources.[88]

And this *is* what was finally clarified, the day Trump stood in the Rose Garden at the White House and triumphantly announced the US withdrawal from the Paris Accord. His statement was a declaration of war authorizing the occupation of all the other countries, if not with troops, at least with $CO_2$, which America retains the right to emit.

Try telling the other signatories of the agreement that they are not literally invaded by the United States, which is influencing the composition of their atmosphere even though they are thousands of kilometers away! Here is a new expression of a *right* to domination in the name of a new version of *Lebensraum*.

Acknowledging that contradictions drive political history, we can see that what fuels the contradiction between the system of production and the system of engendering is dependence on this new form of authority, which is at once very old and freshly minted.

Another difference between the two types of systems is the role attributed to humanity, a direct consequence of this emerging principle of authority. People have been fighting for a century to determine whether questions about nature would make it necessary to exit from anthropocentrism or whether, on the contrary, humans should remain at the center – as if one had to choose between a more or less deep ecology and another more or less "humanistic" version.

Obviously there is no politics other than that of humans, and for their benefit! This has never been in question. The question has always been about the *form* and the *composition of this human.*

What the New Climatic Regime calls into question is not the central place of the human; it is its composition, its presence, its figuration, in a word, its destiny. Now if you modify these things, you also change the definition of human *interests*.

For the Moderns, in effect, it was impossible to situate the human in a precise *landscape*. The term human referred either to a natural being like all the others (in the classical sense of nature-as-universe) or else to the being par excellence capable of extricating itself from nature (again conceived in the old way), thanks to its soul, its culture, or its intelligence. But no one has ever managed to stabilize this oscillation by giving humanity a stable shape.

If the situation is changing today, it is because the climate crisis has driven *both sides* off the rails: the notion of nature on the one hand, that of the human on the other.

What makes the idea of a choice for or against anthropo*centrism* quite implausible is the assumption that there is *a center*, or rather two, man and nature, between which one supposedly has to choose. And even more bizarre is the idea that this circle has such well-defined boundaries that they would leave everything else outside. As if there were an outside!

The issue, under the New Climatic Regime, is precisely that we no longer know on what we depend for subsistence. If decentering is not on the agenda, it is because there is no circle. It is about the Earth much more than about the infinite universe that we must say, after Pascal, that "its center is everywhere and its circumference nowhere."

It is perhaps time, in order to stress this point, to stop speaking about humans and to refer instead to *terrestrials* (the Earthbound), thus insisting on *humus* and, yes, the *compost* included in the etymology of the word "human."[89] ("Terrestrial" has the advantage of not specifying the species.)

Saying "We are earthbound, we are terrestrials amid terrestrials," *does not lead to the same politics as saying* "We are humans in nature." The two are not made of the same cloth – or rather of the same mud.

The third difference between a system of production and a system of engendering has to do with the pos-

86

sibility of multiplying the actors without at the same time *naturalizing behaviors*. To become materialists is no longer to reduce the world to objects, but to extend the list of movements that must be taken into account, precisely the movements of genesis that the view from Sirius did not allow us to follow closely.

Terrestrials in fact have the very delicate problem of discovering how many *other beings* they need in order to subsist. It is by making this list that they sketch out their *dwelling places* (the expression allows us to shift away from the word "territory," a word too often limited to the simple administrative grid of a state).

To track the terrestrials is to add conflicts of interpretation regarding what a given actor is, wants, desires, or can do, to conflicts about what other actors are, want, desire, or can do – and this applies to workers as well as to birds in the sky, to Wall Street executives as well as to bacteria in the soil, to forests as well as to animals.[90] What do you want? What are you capable of? With whom are you prepared to cohabit? Who can threaten you?

We also avoid the trap of thinking that it would be possible to live in sympathy, in harmony, with the so-called "natural" agents. We are not seeking agreement among all these overlapping agents, but we are learning to be dependent on them. No reduction, no harmony. The list of actors simply grows longer; the actors' interests are encroaching on one another; all our powers of investigation are needed if we are to begin to find our place among these other actors.

In a system of engendering, all the agents, all the animated beings, raise questions about descendants and forebears: in short, the question of how to recognize and insert oneself within *lineages* that will manage to last.[91]

The operation is eminently counter-intuitive for the aforementioned Moderns. With them, it was always necessary to choose between the old and the new, which a cleaver had irreversibly separated. The past was no longer what allowed passage, but what was simply surpassed, outdated. To debate this choice, to hesitate, negotiate, take one's time, was to doubt the arrow of time, to be old-fashioned.

The perversity of the modernization front was that, by ridiculing the notion of tradition as archaic, it precluded any form of transmission, inheritance, or revival, and thus of transformation – in short, of engendering. And this is true for the education of human offspring as well as for landscapes, animals, governments, or divinities.

Caught up in a system of production, humans are alone in having the capacity to revolt – always too late; caught up in a system of engendering, *many other protestors* can make themselves heard – before the catastrophe. In the latter system, not only points of view but also points of *life* proliferate.[92]

By shifting from a system of production to a system of engendering, we are going to be able to multiply the sources of revolt against injustice and, consequently, to *increase* considerably the gamut of potential allies in the struggles to come for the Terrestrial.

If such a change in geopolitics stemmed from a philosophical decision, it would have no strength. Before the New Climatic Regime, it seemed, moreover, to be implausible, convoluted, apocalyptic.

From now on, we benefit, so to speak, from help offered by unleashed agents that oblige us to revisit the definition of what it means to be a human, a territory, a politics, a civilization.

The current situation, considered from an oblique angle, is not simply a contradiction, like the countless others that have proliferated in the course of material history within the system of production; it is a contradiction between, on the one hand, the system of production and, on the other, the system of engendering. It is not simply a matter of economics but rather of civilization itself.

To shift from one system to the other we shall have to learn to extricate ourselves from the reign of economization, that view from Sirius that is projected onto the Earth, obscuring it.[93] As Polanyi wrote, the "secular religion" of the market is not *of this world*.[94] Its materialism is an idealism that the climatic mutation has made even more immaterial. To reappropriate the Earth for ourselves is to struggle against invasion by these sorts of extraterrestrials, which have interests and temporalities that differ from those of the infraterrestrials, and which forbid us, literally, to *bring into the world* any being whatsoever.

What has been the object from the beginning of this essay can now be named: the Terrestrial is not yet an *institution*, but it is an actor whose role is clearly different from the political role attributed to "nature" by the Moderns.[95]

The new conflicts do not replace the old ones; they sharpen them, deploy them differently, and above all they finally make them identifiable. Fighting to join one or another utopia, the Global or the Local, does not have the same clarifying effects as fighting to land on Earth!

(By the way, it is perhaps time to stop using the word "ecology" except to designate a scientific field. There are only questions of dwelling places inhabited with or defended against other terrestrials that share the same stakes. The adjective "political" ought to suffice from now on to designate these terrestrials, once the meaning of *polis*, which has for too long restrained the term "political," has been expanded.)

We are at last clearly in a situation of war, but it is a phony war, at once declared and latent.[96] Some people see it everywhere; others ignore it entirely.

Dramatizing somewhat extravagantly, let us call it a conflict between modern humans who believe they are alone in the Holocene, in flight toward the Global or in exodus toward the Local, and the terrestrials who know they are in the Anthropocene and who seek to cohabit with other terrestrials under the authority of a power that as yet lacks any political institution.

And that war, at once civic and moral, divides each of us from within.

## 19.

The Achilles' heel of any text that purports to channel political affects toward new stakes is that the reader can justifiably ask, at the end: "All that is well and good. The hypothesis may be attractive, though it still waits to be proved, but what are we to do with it, practically speaking, and what does it change for me?"

"Do I have to take up permaculture,[97] lead demonstrations,[98] march on the Winter Palace, follow the teachings of St. Francis,[99] become a hacker, organize neighborhood get-togethers, reinvent witches' rites,[100] invest in artificial photosynthesis,[101] or would you rather I track wolves[102]?"

"You say you're giving me a schema for 'triangulating' the positions of my friends and my enemies, but aside from throwing darts to see whether they are moving away or coming closer to one pole or another, I remain completely helpless."

The goal of this essay is certainly not to disappoint, but one cannot ask it to go faster than the history that is under way: the Terrestrial is known by all – who hasn't considered dropping the modernist frame of reference? – and, at the same time, the New Climatic Regime has no institutional embodiment. It is in this in-between position, in this phony war, that we find ourselves, at once mobilized toward the front and demobilized toward the rear.

The situation is all the more uncertain in that the Terrestrial is at once empty and populated. There have been countless initiatives for returning to the soil, a term that is found everywhere – in art exhibits as well as in scientific journals, in the revival of interest in shared resources, in the reoccupation of remote rural areas.[103] Even if, for want of another system of coordinates, we are not aware of this when we go to vote or when we scan the media, everything is already played out: the great displacement has already occurred.[104]

And yet, it is true that the third attractor doesn't look very attractive. It requires too much care, too much attention, too much time, too much diplomacy. Even today it is the Global that shines, that liberates, that arouses enthusiasm, that makes it possible to remain so unaware, that emancipates, that gives the impression of eternal youth. Only it does not exist. It is the Local that reassures, that calms, that offers an identity. But it does not exist either.

The fact remains that the question raised at the beginning of this essay should by now have changed meaning. "How can the feeling of being protected be provided without an immediate return to identity and the defense of borders?" And we can now envisage an answer: "By two complementary movements that modernization has made contradictory: *attaching oneself* to the soil on the one hand, *becoming attached to the world* on the other."

The attractor designated as Terrestrial – which is clearly distinct from "nature" and which is not the entire planet but only the thin biofilm of the Critical Zone – brings together the opposing figures of the soil and the world. A soil that has nothing to do with the Local and a world that resembles neither globalization-minus nor a planetary vision.

From the soil, this attractor inherits materiality, heterogeneity, thickness, dust, humus, the succession of layers, strata, the attentive care that it requires. Everything that cannot be seen from Sirius. Just the opposite of a plot of ground that a development or real estate project has just grabbed. The ground, the soil, in this sense, cannot be appropriated. One belongs to it; it belongs to no one.

But the third attractor also inherits from the world, not in the form of the Global – that globalization-minus associated with the deviation of the modernization project – but in the still active form of the Globe, globalization-plus, that is, the recording of forms of existence that forbid us to limit ourselves to a single location, preclude keeping ourselves inside whatever boundaries there may be.

The soil allows us to attach ourselves; the world allows detachment. Attachment allows us to get away from the illusion of a Great Outside; detachment allows us to escape the illusion of borders. Such is the balancing act to be refined.

What brings us closer to the solution, fortunately, is one of the properties of this new agent of history proper to the New Climatic Regime: one cannot pass from the Local to the Global by moving through a series of interlocking scales, as in the illusory impression of zooming that we can get from Google Earth.[105]

It makes no sense to force the beings animating the struggling territories that constitute the Terrestrial back inside national, regional, ethnic, or identitary boundaries; nor does it make sense to try to withdraw from these territorial struggles so as to "move to the global level" and grasp the Earth "as a whole." The subversion of scales and of temporal and spatial frontiers defines the Terrestrial. This power acts everywhere at once, but it is not unifying. It is political, yes; but it is not statist. It is, literally, atmospheric.

It is in this very practical sense that the Terrestrial reorganizes politics. Each of the beings that participate in the composition of a dwelling place has *its own way* of identifying what is local and what is global, and of defining its entanglements with the others.

$CO_2$ is not spatialized in the same way as urban transport systems; aquifers are not local in the same sense as bird flu; antibiotics globalize the world in a way quite different from that of Islamic terrorists[106]; cities do not form the same spaces as states; the dog Cayenne obliges his mistress, Donna Haraway, to go in directions she would not have anticipated[107]; an economy based on

93

coal, as we have seen, does not shape the same struggles as an economy based on oil. And so on.

The Global and the Local alike afford us an inadequate purchase on the Terrestrial, which explains the current hopelessness: what can be done about problems at once so large and so small? A discouraging prospect, indeed.

What to do? First of all, *generate alternative descriptions*. How could we act politically without having inventoried, surveyed, measured, centimeter by centimeter, being by being, person by person, the stuff that makes up the Earth for us? Without doing this we could perhaps utter astute opinions or defend respectable values, but our political affects would be churning in a void.

Any politics that failed to propose redescribing the dwelling places that have become invisible would be dishonest. We cannot allow ourselves to skip the stage of description. No political lie is more brazen than proposing a program.

If politics has been drained of its substance, it is because the inarticulate complaints of those at the bottom are represented at the top in a form so general and abstract that the two seem to be without common measure. No wonder that politics is accused of a deficit of representation.

But what animate being is capable of describing with any precision the conditions on which it depends? Globalization-minus has made that operation virtually impossible – and indeed this was its main goal: to allow no more footholds for protests, by making it impossible to apprehend the system of production.

Hence the importance of proposing an initial period

of unpacking in order to refine the representation of the landscapes in which the geo-social struggles are situated, before recomposing them. How? As always, from the bottom up, by investigation.

For that, we must agree to define a dwelling place as *that on which a terrestrial depends for its survival*, while asking *what other terrestrials also depend on it?*

It is unlikely that this territory will coincide with a classic legal, spatial, administrative, or geographic entity. On the contrary, the configurations will traverse all scales of space and time.

To define a dwelling place, for a terrestrial, is to list what it needs for its subsistence, and, consequently, what it is *ready to defend*, with its own life if need be. This holds as true for a wolf as for a bacterium, for a business enterprise as for a forest, for a divinity as for a family. What must be documented are the properties of a terrestrial – in all the senses of the word property – by which it is possessed and on which it depends, to the extent that if it were deprived of them, it would disappear.

The challenge obviously lies in drawing up such a list. Here is where the contradiction between the process of production and the process of engendering is most extreme.

In the system of production, the list is easy to make: it consists of humans and resources. In the system of engendering, the task is much more difficult, because the agents, the animate beings, the actors that compose it all have their own trajectories and interests.

A territory, in fact, is not limited to a single type of agent. It encompasses the entire set of animate beings – far away or nearby – whose presence has been determined – by investigation, by experience, by habit, by culture – to be indispensable to the survival of a terrestrial.

It is a matter of broadening the definitions of class by pursuing an exhaustive search for everything that makes subsistence possible. As a terrestrial, what do you care most about? With whom can you live? Who depends on you for subsistence? Against whom are you going to have to fight? How can the importance of all these agents be ranked?

It is when we ask this sort of question that we notice our own ignorance. Every time one begins such an investigation, one is surprised by the abstract nature of the responses. And yet questions about engendering turn up everywhere, along with those of gender, race, education, food, jobs, technological innovations, religion, or leisure. But here's the problem: globalization-minus has made us lose sight, in the literal sense, of the causes and effects of our subjections. Hence the temptation to complain in general, and the impression of no longer having any leverage that could enable us to modify the situation.

People will say that such a redescription of a dwelling place is impossible, that such a political geography is meaningless, that there has never been any such thing.

One episode in French history, however, might give a sense of the undertaking: the construction *of a ledger of complaints*, from January to May 1789, before the revolutionary turn transformed the list of grievances into a question of regime change – monarchy or republic? – and specifically *before* all the descriptions were aggregated to produce the classic conception of Politics as a *totalizing question*. This same view of Politics faces us again today, in the immense and paralyzing question of how to replace capitalism by some other regime.

In a few short months, at the request of a king with his back to the wall, in a situation of financial disaster and climatic tension, all the villages in France, all the cities, all the corporations, not to mention the three estates, managed to describe fairly precisely their living environments, regulation after regulation, plot of ground after plot of ground, privilege after privilege, tax after tax.[108]

Such a description was obviously easier in a period when one could identify more easily than one can today the privileged individuals with whom one came into daily contact, and when one could scan in a single glance the territory that ensured one's subsistence – in the terribly precise sense of staving off famine.

But still, what an exploit! French pupils can still thrill to the narratives of the storming of the Bastille or of Valmy – but the originality of the inscription, of the *geo-graphy* of grievances, is at least as great. In just a few months, moved by the general crisis, stimulated by printed models, a people said to be incompetent proved able to represent for itself the territorial conflicts for which they sought reforms. Existing as a people and being able to describe one's dwelling place is one and the same thing – and this is precisely the capability of which globalization-minus has deprived us. It is for want of territory that there seems to be no body politic.

This episode offers a template for trying to start again, from the bottom up, the description of dwelling places, a template that is all the more impressive in that it seems never to have recurred, at least in France. Is it possible that politics has never done another accounting of its material stakes, at this level of detail, since

97

the pre-Revolutionary epoch? Could we be less capable than our predecessors of defining our interests, our demands, our grievances?

And if that were the reason why politics seemed emptied of all substance, would we not be entirely capable of beginning again? Despite the holes that globalization has dug everywhere, making it very difficult for us to identify our attachments, it is hard to believe that one could not do just as well today.

If it is true that the disappearance of the Global attractor has totally disrupted all the prospects of life for terrestrials (and not only for humans), then we ought to give priority to resuming the work of description on the part of all animate beings. In any case, the experiment is worth attempting.

What is striking in the current situation is the degree to which peoples experiencing deprivation feel disoriented and lost, for want of such a representation of themselves and their interests, and the degree to which they all behave in the same way – those that move and those that stay put, those that emigrate and those that remain behind, those who call themselves "natives" and those who feel like foreigners, as if they have no lasting inhabitable ground under their feet and have to find refuge somewhere.

The question is whether the emergence and description of the Terrestrial attractor can give meaning and direction to political action – forestalling the catastrophe of a headlong flight toward the Local along with the undoing of what has been called the world order. For there to be a world order, there first needs to be a world made more or less shareable by this attempt to take stock.

At the present moment, in mid-2018, onlookers, or at least those who are somewhat sensitive to the situation, are wondering with unconcealed anguish whether it will be possible to avert another August 1914, another suicide – this time worldwide and no longer just European – of nations, under which such a deep depression has been dug that they will all plunge headlong into it – with enthusiasm and delight.

And this time no one will be able to count on the belated support of the United States.

## 20.

After calling for a resumption of the effort to take stock, it would be quite rude not to introduce myself.

An academic from a bourgeois provincial family, a child of the baby boom and thus exactly contemporary with the "Great Acceleration," I have profited greatly from globalization (-plus rather than -minus) without forgetting the plot of land to which I am attached by a family of wine merchants – Burgundy wines that are said to have been globalized since the Gauls! No doubt about it, I am privileged. The reader is free to conclude that I am therefore not qualified to speak of geo-social conflicts.

Among the many attachments that bind me, there are two that I am trying to describe with precision. One has to do with the Critical Zones; it is the object of research that I shall publish later.[109] I would like to conclude these reflections with the other.

To land is necessarily to land someplace. What follows should be taken as an opening in a highly risky diplomatic negotiation with those with whom one wishes to cohabit. In my case, it is in Europe that I want to come down to earth.

Europe, that Old Continent, has changed its geopolitics since the United Kingdom decided it should pull out and since the New World, thanks to Trump, has begun to rigidify into a version of modernity that seems to take the 1950s for its ideal.

It is toward what I hesitate to call the *European homeland* that I should like to turn. Europe is alone, it is true, but only Europe can pick up the thread of its own history. Precisely because it went through August 1914 and dragged the rest of the world along with it. Against globalization and against the return to national and ethnic borders.

Europe's deficiencies are also its strong points. Being an old continent when one is talking about engendering and not simply about production is an advantage, no longer a drawback. It allows us to take up the question of transmission anew. It gives us hope that we might pass from the modern to the *contemporary*.

It is called bureaucratic, this Europe of regulations and wheeling and dealing, the Europe "of Brussels." And yet, as a legal invention, it offers one of the most interesting responses to the once again widespread idea that the nation-state alone can protect peoples by ensuring their safety.

The European Union has managed, through an incredible amount of tinkering, to materialize in countless ways the superimposition and overlapping of the various national interests. It is by the intricacy of its regulations, which are attaining the complexity of an ecosystem, that it shows the way. Exactly the sort of experience that one needs to approach the ecological mutation that is straddling all borders.

The very difficulties the United Kingdom is having as it proceeds to exit from the European Union show the extent to which the construction is original because it has managed to complicate the idea of sovereignty delineated by impermeable borders. Here, then, is one question answered: If the nation-state has long been the vector of modernization leading away from the old affiliations, it is now nothing more than another name for the Local. It is no longer the name of the inhabitable world.

Continental Europe is said to have committed the sin of ethnocentrism and to have claimed to dominate the world, and therefore it has to be "provincialized" to bring it down to size.[110] But this provincialization is saving it today.

Peter Sloterdijk once said that Europe was the club of nations that had definitively given up empire. Let us allow the Brexit supporters, the Trump voters, the Turks, the Chinese, the Russians to keep on harboring their dreams of imperial domination.[111] We know that if they still want to rule over a territory in the cartographic sense, they have no better chances than we have of dominating this Earth that dominates us today just as it dominates them.

Europe knows the fragility of its tenure in global space. No, it can no longer claim to dictate the world order, but it can offer an example of what it means to rediscover inhabitable ground.

After all, it is indeed Europe that claims to have invented the Globe, in the sense of space captured by the instruments of cartography. A system of coordinates so powerful – too powerful – that it makes it possible to record, preserve, and store the multiplicity of life forms. This is the first representation of a common world: simplified, of course, but common; ethnocentric, of course, but common; objectivizing, of course, but common.

Much has been said against this overly cartographic, overly unifying vision of the world, including by me; the fact remains that it is this vision that allows us to consider an initial framework that could enable the relaunching of a diplomatic endeavor.

The fact that Europe has been unable to keep the Globe from slipping through its fingers and from turning into the Global gives it a particular responsibility. It is up to Europe to "de-globalize" this project and thereby to restore its integrity. In spite of everything, it is still Europe's task to redefine the sovereignty of the nation-states – a sovereignty of which Europe invented the model.

Yes, Europe was dangerous when it believed itself capable of "dominating" the world – but wouldn't it be more dangerous still if it shrank down and sought, like a little mouse, to hide itself from history? How could it escape from its vocation of *recalling*, in all senses of the word "recall," the form of modernity that it invented? Precisely because of the crimes it has committed, smallness is not an option.

Among these crimes there is, most important of all, the crime of having believed it could install itself in places, territories, countries, cultures in which it was necessary either to eliminate the inhabitants or to replace their forms of life by its own – in the name of an obligatory "civilization." It is this crime, as we know, that enabled the image and the scientific form of the Globe.

But even that crime is another of its assets: it delivers Europe forever from *innocence*, from the idea that one could either make a new and different history by breaking with the past, or escape from history once and for all.

If the first united Europe was created from below, on a base of coal, iron, and steel, the second will *also come from below*, from the humble matter of a somewhat durable soil. If the first united Europe was created to give a common home to millions of "displaced persons," as was said at the end of the last war, then the second will also be made by and for the displaced persons of today.

Europe has no meaning if it is not in the process of taking another look at the abysses opened up by modernization. This is the best meaning one can give to the idea of a *reflexive* modernization.[112]

In any case, another sense of reflectivity has been imposed on Europe: the backlash of globalization. If this were in danger of being forgotten, the migrations would remind Europe that it cannot escape its past actions.

Europe's wiseacres are indignant: How can so many people think they can cross Europe's borders, settle impudently "in our space" and "make themselves at home"? The anti-immigrationists ought to have thought about this ahead of time, before the "great discoveries," before colonization, before decolonization. Any group that is afraid of the Great Replacement shouldn't have begun by going off to replace "virgin lands" with its own ways of life.

It is as though Europe had made a centennial pact with the potential migrants: we went to your lands without asking your permission; you will come to ours without asking. Give and take. There is no way out of this. Europe has invaded all peoples; all peoples are coming to Europe in their turn.

And besides, Europe has made a pact with the other terrestrials, who are also setting out to invade its borders: the water of the seas, dried-up or overflowing rivers, forests obliged to migrate as fast as possible so as not to be overtaken by climate change, microbes and parasites, all these, too, aspire to a great replacement. We came to you uninvited; you are now coming to us uninvited. We have benefited from every resource; now these resources, having become actors in their own right, have set out, like the Birnam Wood, to recover what belongs to them.

It is in part on Europe's territory that the three great questions of the day can converge:

How can we get out of globalization-minus? How can we come to grips with the earth system's reaction to human actions? How can we organize to welcome the refugees?

This does not mean that others will not do these things. It means that Europe, because of its history, has to plunge in first because it was the first to be responsible.

But what Europe? Who is European? How can the fine expression "dwelling place" be associated with that soulless bureaucratic mechanism?

Europe, soulless? What a misconception! It speaks dozens of languages – and thousands more, thanks to those who have found refuge there. From north to south and from east to west it embraces hundreds of different ecosystems. Everywhere, in every fold of the land, on every street corner, it has traces of the battles that have linked each of its inhabitants with all the others. It has cities – and what cities! Europe is the archipelago of sumptuous cities. Look at them, these cities, and you will understand why people set out from everywhere to have a chance to live in them, even if only on the periphery.

It has knitted together and unraveled in all possible ways the limits and benefits of sovereignty. For centuries it has tasted the bread of democracy. It is small enough not to mistake itself for the world, and big enough not to limit itself to a small plot of ground. It is wealthy, incredibly wealthy, and its wealth is assured by a land that has not been completely ravaged – in part, as we know, because it has invaded and ravaged others!

Almost unbelievably, it has managed to preserve countrysides, landscapes and administrations, and even some welfare states that have not yet been dismantled.

Still another of its advantages is attributable to its vices: having extended its economics to the planet, it has managed not to be completely intoxicated by this phenomenon. Economization is like modernization: it is a poison for export against which Europeans have partially succeeded in protecting themselves by subtle antidotes.

Its limits are not clear? You don't know where it stops? But what terrestrial organism is there about which one can say where it starts and where it stops? Europe is global in its way, like all terrestrials.

It seems that other cultures call it "decadent" and purport to oppose it with their own forms of life. Let them show their virtues, these peoples who do without democracy – and let us let the other peoples judge.

So here we are: Europe is picking up the thread of its history. It wanted to be the whole world. It made a first suicide attempt, and then another. They came close to succeeding. Then it thought it could escape from history by taking shelter under the American umbrella. This umbrella, moral as well as atomic, has been folded up. Europe is alone and without a protector. This is exactly the moment for it to re-enter history without imagining that it will dominate history.[113]

It is a province? Fine; that is just what we need: a local experiment, and yes, a provincial experiment in what it means to inhabit an earth *after* modernization, *with those* whom modernization has definitively displaced.

As it did at the beginning of its history, Europe is again taking up the question of universality, but this time it is not rushing to impose its own prejudices on everyone else.

There is nothing like an Old Continent for taking up on a new basis what is common, while observing, with anguish, that the universal condition today entails living in the ruins of modernization, groping for a dwelling place.

After all, going back to the question of the common world at the moment of an unanticipated return to barbarism, when those who constituted the old "West" have abandoned the very idea of building a world order – isn't this actually a more positive version of its age-old history?

The Earth that Europe had wanted to grasp as a Globe is offering itself anew as the Terrestrial, offering Europe *a second chance that it in no way deserved.* This is quite fitting for the region of the world that has the greatest responsibility in the history of the ecological upheaval. One more weakness that may become an advantage.

How could one doubt that Europe may become one of the homelands of all those who are looking for ground? "A European is anyone who wants to be one." I would like to be proud of it, of this Europe, with all its wrinkles and seams; I would like to be able to call it my homeland – their refuge.

There, I've finished. Now, if you wish, it's your turn to present yourself, tell us a little about where you would like to land and with whom you agree to share a dwelling place.

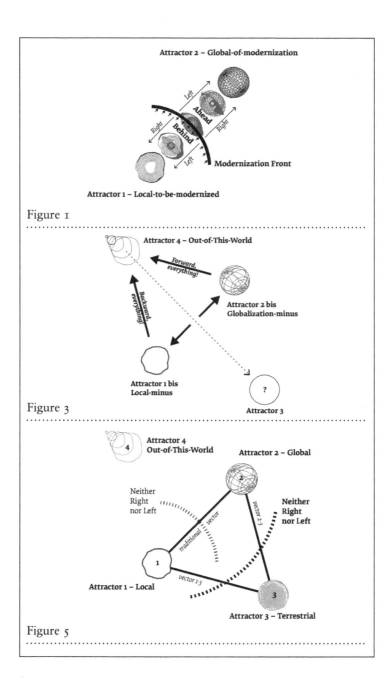

Figure 1

Attractor 2 – Global-of-modernization

Left

Ahead

Right

Behind

Right

Left

Modernization Front

Attractor 1 – Local-to-be-modernized

Figure 3

Attractor 4 – Out-of-This-World

Forward, everything!

Backward, everything!

Attractor 2 bis
Globalization-minus

Attractor 1 bis
Local-minus

?

Attractor 3

Figure 5

Attractor 4
Out-of-This-World

Attractor 2 – Global

Neither
Right
nor Left

traditional vector

Neither
Right
nor Left

vector 2-3

Attractor 1 – Local

vector 1-3

Attractor 3 – Terrestrial

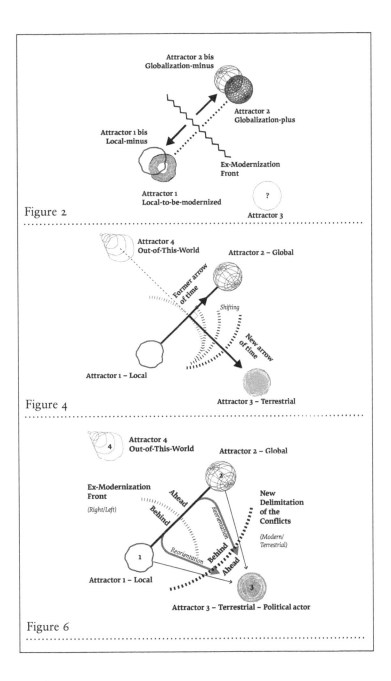

**Figure 2**

Attractor 2 bis
Globalization-minus

Attractor 2
Globalization-plus

Attractor 1 bis
Local-minus

Ex-Modernization
Front

Attractor 1
Local-to-be-modernized

?
Attractor 3

**Figure 4**

Attractor 4
Out-of-This-World

Attractor 2 – Global

Former arrow
of time

Shifting

New arrow
of time

Attractor 1 – Local

Attractor 3 – Terrestrial

**Figure 6**

Attractor 4
Out-of-This-World

Attractor 2 – Global

Ex-Modernization
Front

(Right/Left)

Ahead

Behind

Reorientation

New
Delimitation
of the
Conflicts

(Modern/
Terrestrial)

Reorientation

Behind

Ahead

Attractor 1 – Local

Attractor 3 – Terrestrial – Political actor

# Notes

1 Remark made by Donald Trump's son-in-law, cited by Sarah Vowell, *The New York Times,* August 8, 2017.
2 See in particular Francis Fukayama, *The End of History and the Last Man* (New York: Free Press, 1992).
3 The expression "New Climatic Regime" is developed in Bruno Latour, *Facing Gaia: Eight Lectures on the New Climatic Regime,* trans. Catherine Porter (Cambridge, MA: Harvard University Press, 2017 [2015]).
4 Catholics have done everything they could to ignore the link between poverty and ecological disasters that is clearly articulated, however, in Pope Francis's encyclical, *Laudato Si!* (Vatican: Holy See, 2015).
5 Even French President Macron, who has been indifferent to these questions, felt obliged to take them in hand when he introduced #MaketheEarthGreatAgain barely two days after Trump's announcement.

6 Dina Ionesco, Daria Mokhnacheva, and François Gemenne, *The Atlas of Environmental Migration* (London: Routledge, 2016).

7 See Stefan Aykut and Amy Dahan, *Gouverner le climat? Vingt ans de négociation climatique* (Paris: Presses de Sciences Po, 2015). The text of the INDC (Intended Nationally Determined Contribution, in UN jargon) that had been prepared for COP21 presents each country's development projects (see www.diplomatie.gouv.fr/fr/politique-etrangere-de-la-france/climat/paris-205-cop21/les-contributions-nationales-pour-la-cop-21, accessed August 7, 2017).

8 The wicked universality of losing one's property is well documented in Saskia Sassen, *Expulsions: Brutality and Complexity in the Global Economy* (Cambridge, MA: Harvard University Press, 2014).

9 Hence the aptness of the expression "learning how to live in the ruins," from Anna Lowenhaupt Tsing's very important book, *The Mushroom at the End of the World: On the Possibility of Life in Capitalist Ruins* (Princeton, NJ: Princeton University Press, 2015).

10 The idea of a modernization front and the way it parcels out political affects is developed more fully in Bruno Latour, *We Have Never Been Modern*, trans. Catherine Porter (Cambridge, MA: Harvard University Press, 1993 [1991]).

11 Karl Polanyi, *The Great Transformation* (Boston, MA: Beacon Press, 1957 [1944]).

12 This text follows a convention according to which the lower-case term "earth" corresponds to the

traditional framework of human activity (human beings in nature), while the upper-case "Earth" indicates a power to act in which we begin to recognize, even if it has not been fully instituted, something like a political entity.

13 On this history, see especially Paul N. Edwards, *A Vast Machine: Computer Models, Climate Data, and the Politics of Global Warming* (Cambridge, MA: MIT Press, 2010).

14 See Christophe Bonneuil and Jean-Baptiste Fressoz, *The Shock of the Anthropocene: The Earth, History and Us*, trans. David Fernbach (New York: Verso, 2016).

15 See Naomi Oreskes and Erik M. Conway, *Merchants of Doubt: How a Handful of Scientists Obscured the Truth on Issues from Tobacco Smoke to Global Warming* (New York: Bloomsbury Press, 2010).

16 This dating is obviously quite vague, but it does not contradict the data provided by Thomas Piketty in *Capital in the Twenty-First Century*, trans. Arthur Goldhammer (Cambridge, MA: Harvard University Press, 2014 [2013]), and the very meticulous exploration by Dominique Pestre of the way economics has absorbed and euphemized ecology. See especially Dominique Pestre, "La mise en économie de l'environnement comme règle, 1970–2010. Entre théologie économique, pragmatisme et hégémonie politique," *Ecologie et Politique* 52 (2016): 19–44. The reactions to the 1972 Club of Rome report can serve as a milestone in this whole business of chronology. See Élodie Vieille-Blanchard, "Les limites à la croissance dans un monde global.

Modélisations, prospectives, réfutations," thesis, EHESS, Paris, 2011.

17 In *The World Inequality Report: 2018* (Cambridge, MA: Belknap Press, 2018), Facundo Alvaredo et al. confirm that the turning point is around the 1980s, as was shown so brilliantly in David Leonhardt, "Our Broken Economy, in One Simple Chart," *The New York Times*, August 7, 2017.

18 For an astonishing psychological portrait of the Titanic's owner, who survived the shipwreck, see Frances Wilson, *How to Survive the Titanic: The Sinking of J. Bruce Ismay* (New York: Harper, 2012).

19 See David Kaiser and Lee Wasserman, "The Rockefeller Family Fund Takes on Exxon Mobil," *New York Review of Books*, December 8 and 22, 2016. See also Geoffrey Supran and Naomi Oreskes, "Assessing Exxon Mobil's Climate Change Communications (1977–2014)," *Environmental Research Letters* 12, no. 8 (2017).

20 See Evan Osnos, "Doomsday Prep for the Super-Rich," *The New Yorker* (January 30, 2017): https://www.newyorker.com/magazine/2017/01/30/dooms day-prep-for-the-super-rich. For a striking portrait of the building of this offshore world, see the Paradise Papers published by the *International Consortium for Investigative Journalism* in 2017: https://www.icij.org/investigations/paradise-papers/.

21 The problem with conspiracy theories, as Luc Boltanski has shown, is that they sometimes correspond all too well to reality (Luc Boltanski, *Mysteries and Conspiracies*, trans. Catherine

Porter [Cambridge, UK: Polity, 2014]). It is tempting to believe this if one reads Nancy MacLean's *Democracy in Chains: The Deep History of the Radical Right's Stealth Plan for America* (London: Penguin Random House, 2017).

22 This is the common tenet of sociology of science and technology (STS). See, for instance, Ulrike Felt et al., *The Handbook of Science and Technology Studies*, 4th edn (Cambridge, MA: MIT Press, 2016).

23 See James Hoggan, *Climate Cover-Up: The Crusade to Deny Global Warming* (Vancouver: Greystone Books, 2009).

24 See the very short and very disturbing book by Naomi Oreskes and Erik M. Conway, *The Collapse of Western Civilization: A View from the Future* (New York: Columbia University Press, 2014).

25 This does not mean that commentators are aware of it. In a manifesto published in book form in 12 languages that brings together what intellectuals have to say about the "great regression" – in other words, the surprise they feel at the "rise of populism" – only one chapter, mine, deals with this question: see Heinrich Geiselberger, ed. *The Great Regression* (London: Polity, 2017).

26 Marshall Sahlins, *Culture in Practice* (New York: Zone Books, 2000).

27 See the site of Singularity University, https://su.org, accessed August 7, 2017, and for a frightening description, see Yuval Noah Harari, *Homo Deus: A Brief History of Tomorrow* (London: Harvill Secker, 2016).

28 The multiplication, on the left as well as on the

right, of more and more strident demands for identity politics in the name of non-negotiable values shows that the second pole, that of the Globe, has ceased to exercise the power of attraction that once made it possible to fuse the two in a project of universality.

29 I thank Jean-Michel Frodon for this link to the film *Sully* (2016).

30 This is different from conservative thinking, as Jeremy W. Peters suggests in "They're Building a Trump-centric Movement. But Don't Call It Trumpism" (*The New York Times*, August 5, 2017).

31 Only at the very end of the twentieth century did the issue of the climate become as essential a theme defining Republicans as abortion or anti-Darwinism. The strategy of Trump's appointee as director of the Environmental Protection Agency, Scott Pruitt, aimed at obliterating knowledge about climate questions, seems to follow a more coherent policy than that of the president.

32 Offshoring had existed as an important sociological phenomenon (see John Urry, *Offshoring* [London: Polity, 2014]) but it was not meant to be practiced by a whole nation!

33 This is what Kyle McGee calls "heathen"; see *Heathen Earth: Trumpism and Political Ecology* (Goleta, CA: Punctum Books, 2017).

34 As was done in *Facing Gaia*, 2017.

35 The theme of geohistory was introduced in a well-known article by Dipesh Chakrabarty, "The Climate of History: Four Theses," *Critical Inquiry* 35 (Winter 2009): 197–222.

36 See Anna Lowenhaupt Tsing, Nils Bubandt, Elaine Ganet, and Heather Anne Swanson, eds., *Arts of Living on a Damaged Planet: Ghosts and Monsters of the Anthropocene* (Minneapolis, MN: University of Minnesota Press, 2017).

37 This figure of the modern mind undergoing retraining was sketched by Michel Tournier with his Crusoe to whom Friday has to explain patiently how to behave on his island in order to stop being a stranger, as he was at first. Another inversion of the ties between possessor and property, so complete that Crusoe decides in the end to remain on Speranza Island! See Michel Tournier, *Friday*, trans. Norman Denny (New York: Pantheon Books, 1969 [1967]).

38 See Clive Hamilton, Christophe Bonneuil, and François Gemenne, *The Anthropocene and the Global Environmental Crisis: Rethinking Modernity in a New Epoch* (London: Routledge, 2015).

39 See the remarkable presentation in Timothy Lenton, *Earth System Science* (Oxford: Oxford University Press, 2016).

40 Hence the lively dispute over the comeback – or not – of the human figure as principal actor. To take two extremes: Donna Haraway, *Staying with the Trouble: Making Kin in the Chthulucene* (Durham, NC: Duke University Press, 2016), and Clive Hamilton, *Defiant Earth: The Fate of Humans in the Anthropocene* (Cambridge, UK: Polity, 2017).

41 I thank Aurélien Gamboni and Sandrine Tuxeido for making this connection between Poe's tale and the climate crisis.

42 See www.globalwitness.org/en/campaigns/environ mental-activists/dangerous-ground, accessed August 7, 2017.

43 From Blair to Macron. But also, more seriously in social theory. See Anthony Giddens, *Beyond Left and Right: The Future of Radical Politics* (London: Polity, 1994).

44 This is the problem of the affects triggered by the theme of de-growth. On the modern horizon, one cannot adopt de-growth without regressing. Or else one has to change horizons. Hence the importance of proposing other terms, perhaps that of *prosperity*. Along the new vector, if one cannot progress, at least one may hope to *prosper*.

45 Anna Tsing has offered a better schema than this one; hers consists in taking any stake at all as being tugged in different directions by the four attractors. This would indeed be more realistic, but harder to present in a simple drawing. Personal communication, Aarhus, June 2016.

46 See Bruno Latour and Peter Weibel, *Making Things Public: Atmospheres of Democracy* (Cambridge, MA: MIT Press, 2005).

47 See Noortje Marres, *Material Participation: Technology, the Environment and Everyday Publics* (London: Palgrave, 2012). It is to Marres that we owe the fine slogan: "No issue, no politics."

48 The acronym ZAD for the French *Zones à défendre* has given rise to "zadist" as a label for activists who are trying to stop the construction of an airport near the city of Nantes. Their strategy has been to occupy the land to be "developed" for the

projected airport and to ally themselves in new ways with farmers and other activists.

49 According to the neologism offered by Donna Haraway to distinguish the world from the globe of globalization.

50 The difficulties that the sociologists of the social have simply locating the sociology of associations (also called actor network theory or ANT) provide in a reduced form an almost perfect parallel with the slowness of the socialist movements in figuring out how to deal with ecological questions. Let us recall that "collective" is the term that can replace "social" while extending the range of associations that are thus *collected*. See Bruno Latour, *Reassembling the Social: An Introduction to Actor-Network Theory* (Oxford: Oxford University Press, 2005).

51 The term signals the exponential growth of the impact of human activity on the planet, conventionally deemed to have begun in the wake of the Second World War. See Will Steffen, Wendy Broadgate, Lisa Deutsch, Owen Gaffney, and Cornelia Ludwig, "The Trajectory of the Anthropocene: The Great Acceleration," *The Anthropocene Review* 2 (2015): 81–98.

52 A blockage further highlighted by the continual complaints about "the end of the revolutionary spirit," about the need to "invent new utopias" or to propose "new mobilizing myths" – so many ways of continuing to dream aloud of the same historical trajectory.

53 See Pierre Charbonnier, "Le socialisme est-il une politique de la nature? Une lecture écologique

de Karl Polanyi," *Incidences* 11 (2015): 183–204.

54 Here I am returning to the question raised by Naomi Klein's title, *This Changes Everything: Capitalism vs. the Climate* (New York: Simon & Schuster, 2014), trying to understand just why so few things are changing because of the stability of political reference points – and in particular because of the numbing effect of the term capitalism.

55 Or else they are not managing to exit from a model that naturalizes the question once again. This is the problem of any biological metaphor, such as "metabolism." Hence the importance of going back upstream to reconsider the notions of nature so as to be sure that they are not going to extinguish precisely the politics that some were seeking to relaunch. See Jason Moore, *Capitalism in the Web of Life: Ecology and the Accumulation of Capital* (New York: Verso, 2015); the book's title restates succinctly the problem that I am trying to circumscribe here.

56 Timothy Mitchell, *Carbon Democracy: Political Power in the Age of Oil* (London: Verso, 2011).

57 Trump's obsession with a return to coal ("King Coal") is an almost perfect illustration of the new geopolitics: a dreamed-of smoking utopia with all the associated social relationships on an earth that no longer exists and in an epoch outdated by 50 years.

58 A link forcefully pursued for many years by Mike Davis, e.g., *Late Victorian Holocausts: El Niño Famines and the Making of the Third World* (London: Verso, 2002).

59 I am borrowing this contrast from Michel Lussault, *De la lutte des classes à la lutte des places* (Paris: Fayard, 2009), but in a somewhat different sense, as will become clear later on. I recognize that "geo-social" maintains the dualism and makes the hyphen do all the work. This is a case in which we need to put new wine in old skins.

60 Cited in www.reporterre.net/Nous-ne-defendons-pas-la-nature, accessed August 7, 2017.

61 Bruno Latour, *Politics of Nature: How to Bring the Sciences into Democracy*, trans. Catherine Porter (Cambridge, MA: Harvard University Press, 2004).

62 The whole point of Timothy Mitchell's *Carbon Democracy* is to make clear how a science of scarcity was turned into a science of boundless cornucopia. There is a pattern here: when ecology insists on the existence of limits, economic sciences find a way to invent a limitless future.

63 Leaving to one's grandchildren a world less inhabited than the one into which they were born, living with the idea that one is an agent of the sixth extinction – these are some of the preoccupations that tilt all ecological questions into tragedy.

64 The term was introduced by Edmund Husserl. The theme of the infinite universe goes back to the classic work of Alexandre Koyré, *From the Closed World to the Infinite Universe* (Baltimore, MD: Johns Hopkins University Press, 1957).

65 See the magnificent three-volume work edited by Dominique Pestre, *L'histoire des sciences et des savoirs* (Paris: Seuil, 2015). This collection succeeds in historicizing the producers

of universality and especially in situating them geographically.

66 See Isabelle Stengers, *The Invention of Modern Science*, trans. Daniel L. Smith (Minneapolis, MN: University of Minnesota Press, 2000 [1993]).

67 See Isabelle Stengers, *La vierge et le neutrino* (Paris: Les Empêcheurs de penser en rond, 2005), especially the annex.

68 The paradox is that a machine in no way obeys the principles of mechanics, which remain a form of idealism; Gilbert Simondon developed this theme in *On the Mode of Existence of Technical Objects*, trans. Cecile Malaspina and John Rogove (Minneapolis, MN: Univocal Publishing, 2017). That machines are not mechanistically made is shown in Bruno Latour, *Aramis, or the Love of Technology*, trans. Catherine Porter (Cambridge, MA: Harvard University Press, 1996).

69 In *Nature as Event: The Lure of the Possible*, trans. Michael Halewood (Durham, NC: Duke University Press, 2017), Didier Debaise gives a particularly illuminating version of the philosophical history of this bifurcation.

70 The term "naturalist" has been defined in a now canonical way by Philippe Descola in *Beyond Nature and Culture*, trans. Janet Lloyd (Chicago, IL: University of Chicago Press, 2013).

71 See Silvia Federici, *Caliban and the Witch* (New York: Autonomedia, 2004).

72 An obsession on the part of reactionary thought with the risks posed by migrations that would come in and replace a people autochthonous "by birth" with an allochthonous group. Like all popular

obsessions, this one symbolizes and displaces the presence of another phenomenon, another great replacement: the change of land.

73 Hence the effort to make the contrast between Planet and Terrestrial visible thanks to cartography, as in the project undertaken by Frédérique Aït-Touati, Alexandra Arènes, and Axelle Grégoire, *Terra Forma*. See http://cargocollective.com/ether restrategiclandscape/TERRA-FORMA

74 Hence the importance of the second and less-well-known part of Descola's *Beyond Nature and Culture* on modes of relation, especially the passages on production.

75 An abrupt transformation of the gaze which makes us read as avidly Nastasja Martin, *Les âmes sauvages: Face à l'Occident, la résistance d'un people d'Alaska* (Paris: La Découverte, 2016) as Anna Lowenhaupt Tsing's stunning *The Mushroom at the End of the World*.

76 See Sébastien Dutreuil, "Gaïa: Hypothèse, programme de recherche pour le système terre, or philosophie de la nature?" (doctoral thesis, University of Paris I, 2016); a book is forthcoming. See also Bruno Latour, *Facing Gaia*, and Timothy Lenton, *Earth System*.

77 James Lovelock, *The Ages of Gaia: A Biography of Our Living Earth* (New York: Norton, 1995).

78 This point has been developed further in Bruno Latour, "Why Gaia is not a God of Totality," special issue, "Geosocial Formations and the Anthropocene," *Theory, Culture and Society* 34.2–3 (2017): 61–82.

79 Alexander von Humboldt's return to favor is

a symptom of this shift toward the earth sciences differently conceived. See Andrea Wulf's best-seller, *The Invention of Nature: Alexander von Humboldt's New World* (New York: Knopf, 2015).

80 This scenario of metaphorical teleportation is explored among others in the survey proposed by Déborah Danowski and Eduardo Viveiros de Castro in *The Ends of the World*, trans. Rodrigo Nunes (Cambridge, UK: Polity, 2016).

81 This term is used by a network of researchers in earth science to compare equipped sites – often in catchment basins – by combining the results of disciplines that previously worked separately (http://criticalzone.org/national/). In the singular, the term Critical Zone designates the thin layer in which life has radically modified the earth's atmosphere and geology – as opposed either to the space beyond or to the deep geology below. See Susan L. Brantley et al., "Designing a Network of Critical Zone Observatories to Explore the Living Skin of the Terrestrial Earth," *Earth Surface Dynamics* 5 (2017): 841–60.

82 A major part of Isabelle Stengers' work lies in slowing down that disqualification but without diminishing the importance of the sciences: this is what she calls "civilizing." See her recent *In Catastrophic Times: Resisting the Coming Barbarism*, trans. Andrew Goffey (London: Open Humanities Press, 2015).

83 Examples abound, but see especially Charles D. Keeling, "Rewards and Penalties of Recording the Earth," *Annual Review of Energy and*

*Environment* 23 (1998): 25–82, and Michael E. Mann, *The Hockey Stick and the Climate Wars: Dispatches from the Front Lines* (New York: Columbia University Press, 2013).

84 The idea of an active production of ignorance has been popularized in the case of tobacco by Robert Proctor, in *Golden Holocaust: Origins of the Cigarette Catastrophe and the Case for Abolition* (Berkeley, CA: University of California Press, 2011).

85 "The communist question has been badly framed, first because it has been raised as a *social question*, that is, as a *strictly human* question. Despite this, it has never stopped disrupting the world." Comité Invisible, *Maintenant* (Paris: La Fabrique, 2017), p. 127.

86 See Will Steffens et al., "Planetary Boundaries: Guiding Human Development on a Changing Planet," *Science Express*, 2015.

87 The myth of American Republicans according to which climate science is a Socialist or Chinese plot to dominate the United States provides a quite explicit figure for this power, recognized as intentional and directly geopolitical – indicating that the adherents to an alternative reality are, in spite of everything, capable of designating with a certain precision the reality that they are confronting.

88 Clive Hamilton's *Defiant Earth* raises the important question of a necessary return to anthropocentrism.

89 Suggested in Haraway, *Staying with the Trouble*, p. 55.

90 The success of works that reveal the agency of

beings as different as forests, intestinal bacteria, chimpanzees, mushrooms, or soils, attests to the great swerve in the definition of what acts. It is this change of paradigm that Vinciane Despret has documented so well. See, in particular, *What Would Animals Say If We Asked the Right Questions?*, trans. Brett Buchanan (Minneapolis, MN: University of Minnesota Press, 2016 [2012]).

91 Hence the importance of the philosophy of the organism developed by Whitehead and renewed by Isabelle Stengers in *Thinking with Whitehead: A Free and Wild Creation of Concepts*, trans. Michael Chase (Cambridge, MA: Harvard University Press, 2011 [2002]).

92 The term *point de vie* (in French, it nicely parallels *point de vue*) has been proposed by Emanuele Coccia in *La vie des plantes: Une métaphysique du mélange* (Paris: Payot, 2016).

93 See Michael Callon, *L'emprise des marchés: Comprendre leur fonctionnement pour pouvoir les changer* (Paris: La Découverte, 2017), a development of his earlier *Laws of the Market* (Oxford: Blackwell, 1998).

94 Polanyi, *The Great Transformation*, p. 139.

95 Here, in a sense, we come back to the old word "law" as Montesquieu understood it; he linked it explicitly, moreover, to the notion of "climate." This term, long misunderstood itself until the advent of the New Climatic Regime, would oblige us to write something like "the spirit of the laws of nature." I am grateful to Gerard de Vries for his interpretation of Montesquieu.

96 Hence the weirdness of watching Macron and

Trump together saluting the troops parading along the Champs-Elysées on July 14, 2017.

97 As many people have done after seeing the documentary film by Cyril Dion and Mélanie Laurent, *Tomorrow*, produced by Bruno Levy, 2015: https:// www.tomorrow-documentary.com.

98 The text by the "Comité invisible [Invisible Committee]," *Maintenant*, which is at once revolutionary and bizarrely full of Christian spirituality, offers little in the way of practical conclusions beyond "smashing some cops" in order to take the lead in demonstrations.

99 Readers may recall that *Empire*, a book by Michael Hardt and Tony Negri (Paris: UGE, 2004), ended curiously by praising St. Francis.

100 See Starhawk, *Parcours d'une altermondialiste: De Seattle aux Twin Towers*, trans. Isabelle Stengers and Édith Rubenstein (Paris: Les Empêcheurs de penser en rond, 2004).

101 By investing in the magnificent project of Marc Robert and his group; see the article by Heng Rao, Luciana C. Schmidt, Julien Bonin, and Marc Robert, "Visible-Light-Driven Methane Formation from $CO_2$ with a Molecular Iron Catalyst," *Nature* 548 (2017): 74–7.

102 As in the project outlined by Baptiste Morizot, *Les Diplomates: Cohabiter avec les loups sur une nouvelle carte du vivant* (Marseille: Wildproject, 2016).

103 A typical example is the success of the Soil Care Network created by Anna Krzywoszyńska, https:// www.soilcarenetwork.com.

104 See Marie Cornu, Fabienne Orsi, and Judith

Rochfeld, eds., *Dictionnaire des biens communs* (Paris: PUF, 2017).

105 This anti-zoom standpoint is an essential aspect of actor-network theory; see Valérie November, Eduardo Camacho-Hübner, and Bruno Latour, "Entering a Risky Territory: Space in the Age of Digital Navigation," *Environment and Planning D: Society and Space* 28 (2010): 581–99.

106 See Hannah Landecker, "Antibiotic Resistance and the Biology of History," *Body and Society* (2015): 1–34. I thank Charlotte Brives for bringing this astonishing article to my attention.

107 Donna Haraway, *The Companion Species Manifesto: Dogs, People, and Significant Otherness* (Chicago, IL: Prickly Paradigm Press, 2003).

108 See Philppe Grateau, *Les Cahiers de doléances: Une lecture culturelle* (Rennes: Presses Universitaires de Rennes, 2001).

109 Bruno Latour, "Some Advantages of the Notion of 'Critical Zone' for Geopolitics," special issue, "Geochemistry of the Earth's Surface, GES-10, Paris, France, 18–23 August, 2014," *Procedia Earth and Planetary Science* 10 (2014): 3–6.

110 Dipesh Chakrabarty, *Provincializing Europe: Postcolonial Thought and Historical Difference* (Princeton, NJ: Princeton University Press, 2008 [2000]).

111 Peter Sloterdijk, *Si l'Europe s'éveille* (Paris: Mille et une nuits, 2003 [1995]).

112 The term was introduced in a different sense by Ulrich Beck, Anthony Giddens, and Scott Lash, *Reflexive Modernization: Politics, Tradition and*

*Aesthetics in the Modern Social Order* (Stanford, CA: Stanford University Press, 1994).

113 As Angela Merkel put it after Trump abandoned the Paris Accord, on May 28, 2017: "We Europeans must take charge of our own fate."